HAPPINESS
COLORING BOOK

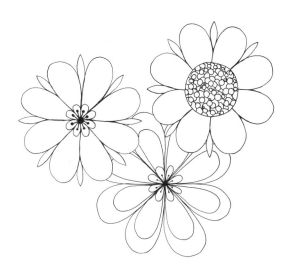

HAPPINESS
COLORING BOOK

Delightful images to brighten your mood

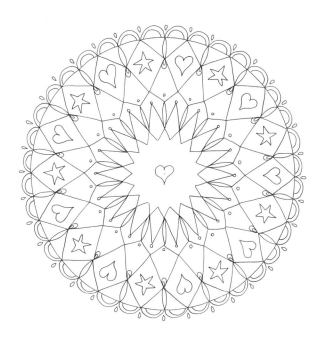

Andrea Sargent

CHARTWELL
BOOKS

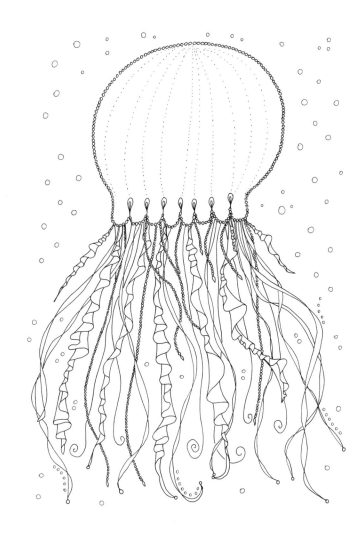

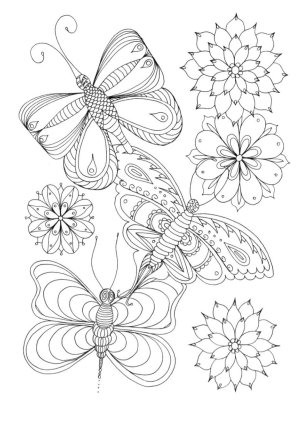

This edition published in 2016 by
CHARTWELL BOOKS
an imprint of Book Sales
a division of Quarto Publishing Group USA Inc.
142 West 36th Street, 4th Floor
New York, New York 10018
USA

Copyright © Arcturus Holdings Limited/Andrea Sargent

Arcturus Publishing Limited,
26/27 Bickels Yard, 151–153 Bermondsey Street,
London SE1 3HA

ISBN: 978-0-7858-3416-8
CH004964NT

Printed in China

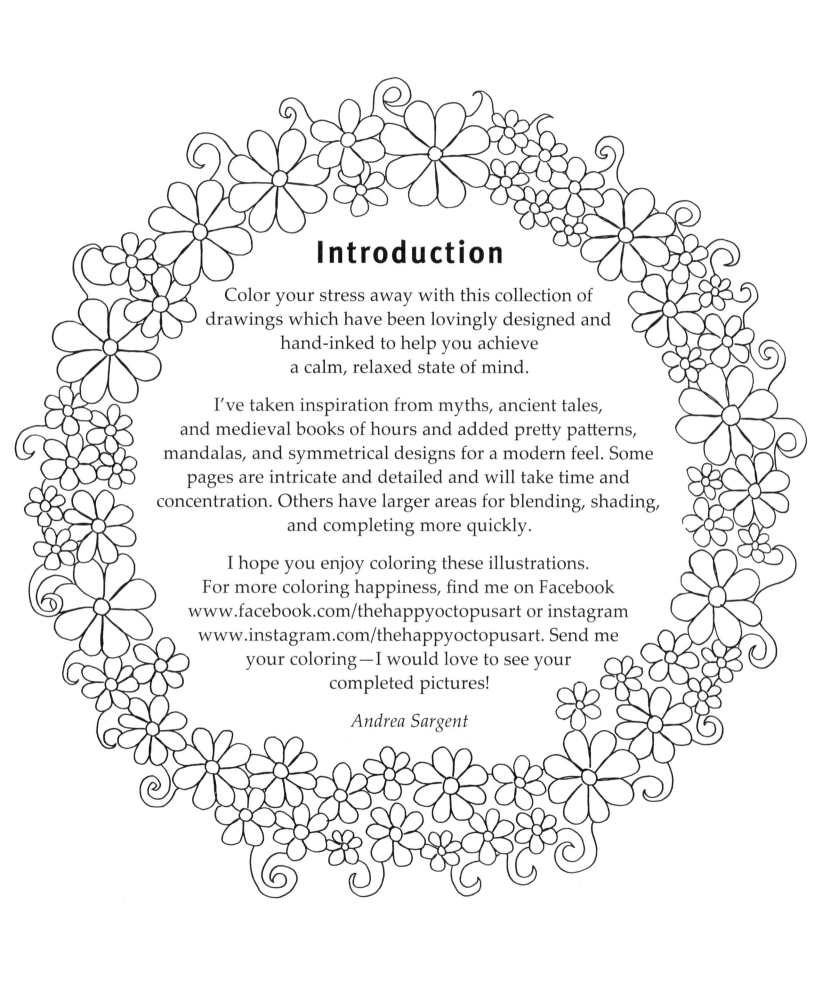

Introduction

Color your stress away with this collection of
drawings which have been lovingly designed and
hand-inked to help you achieve
a calm, relaxed state of mind.

I've taken inspiration from myths, ancient tales,
and medieval books of hours and added pretty patterns,
mandalas, and symmetrical designs for a modern feel. Some
pages are intricate and detailed and will take time and
concentration. Others have larger areas for blending, shading,
and completing more quickly.

I hope you enjoy coloring these illustrations.
For more coloring happiness, find me on Facebook
www.facebook.com/thehappyoctopusart or instagram
www.instagram.com/thehappyoctopusart. Send me
your coloring—I would love to see your
completed pictures!

Andrea Sargent

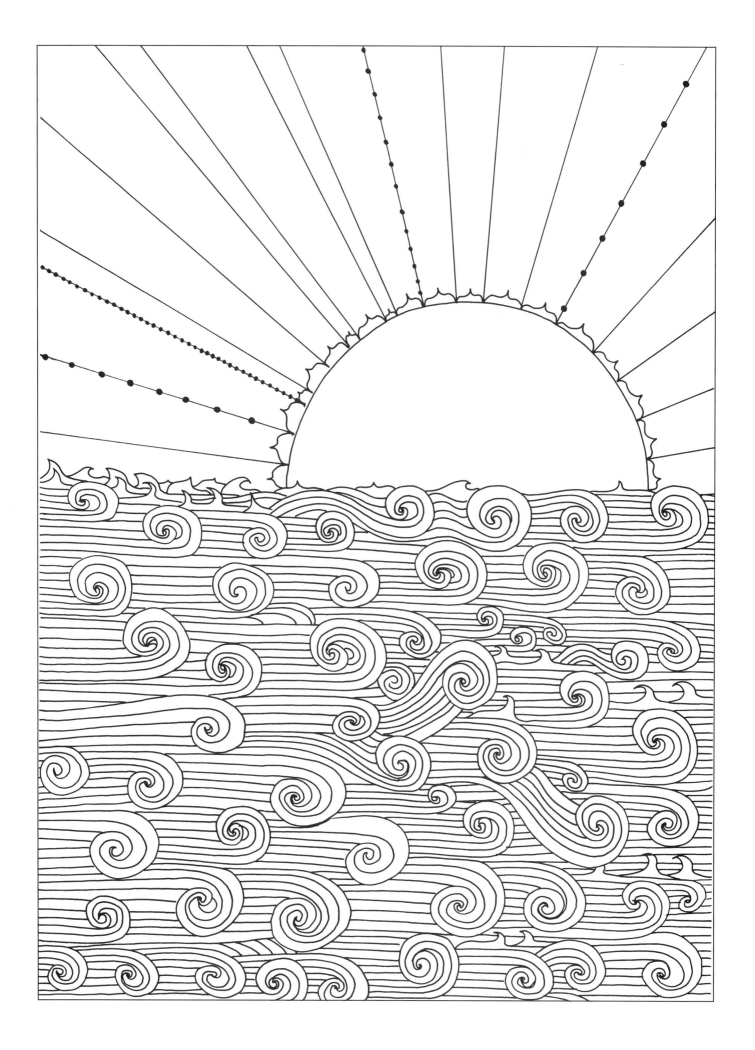

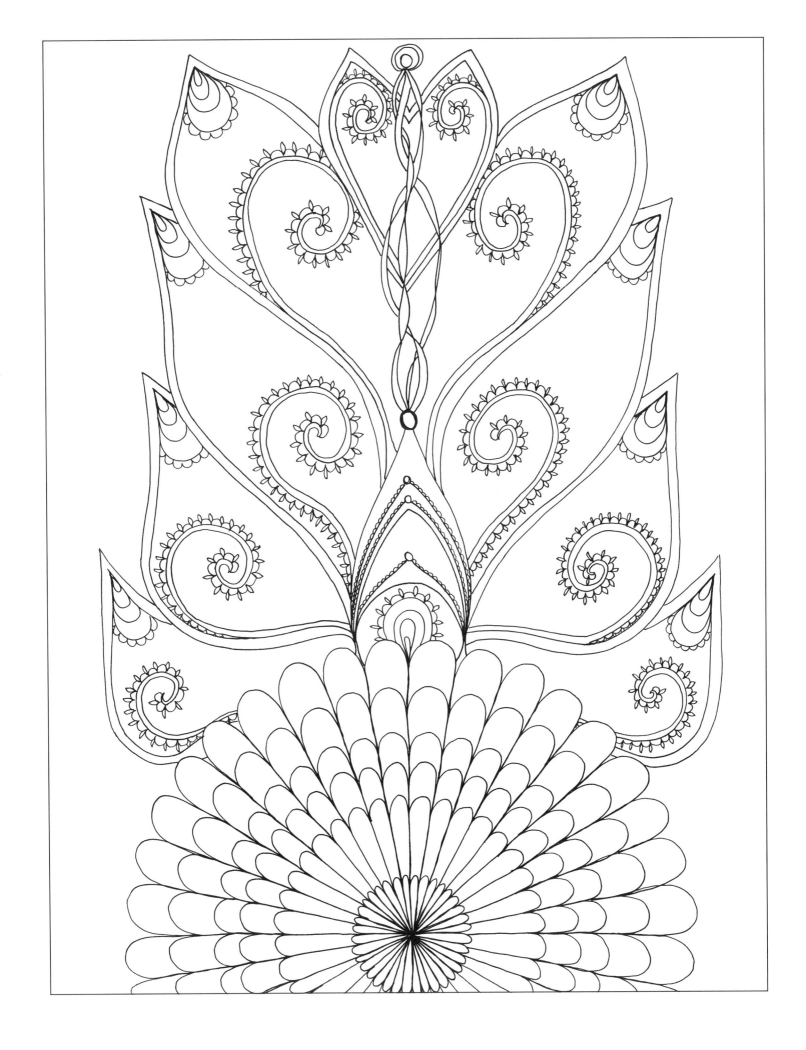

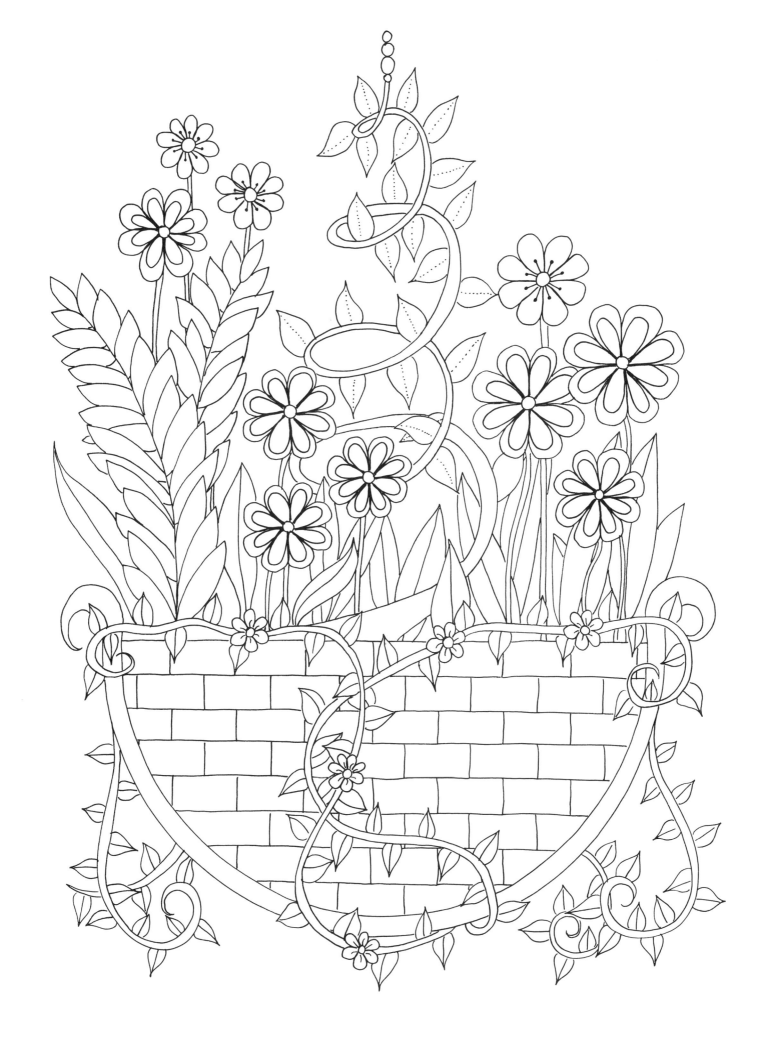

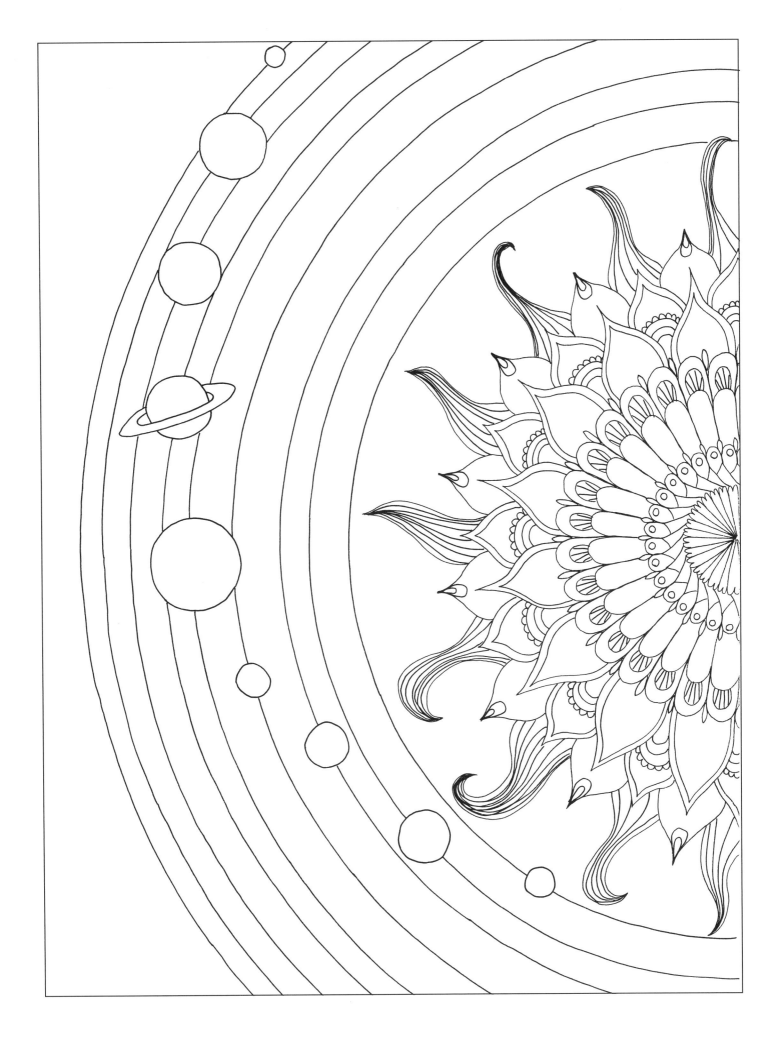

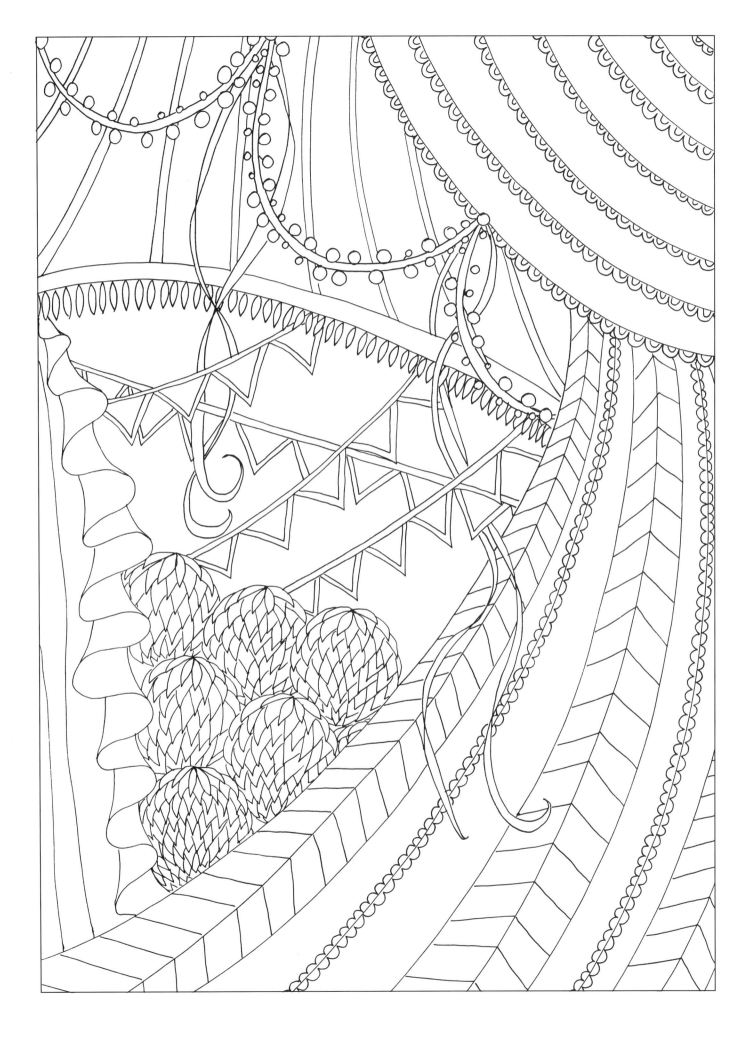

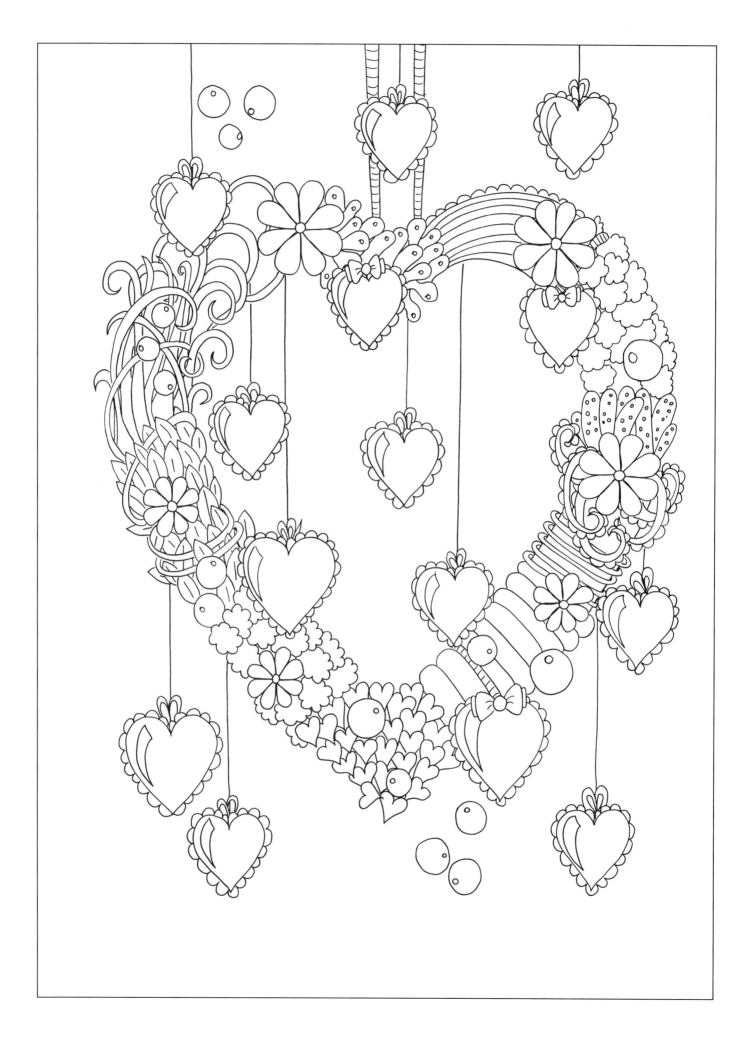

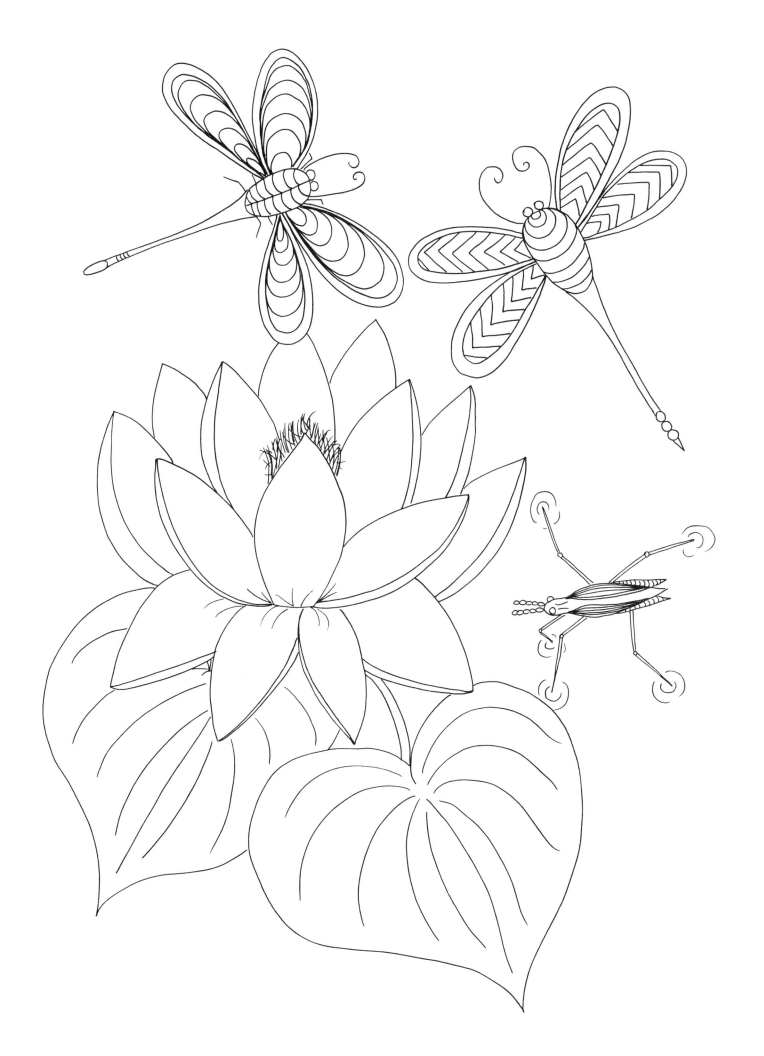

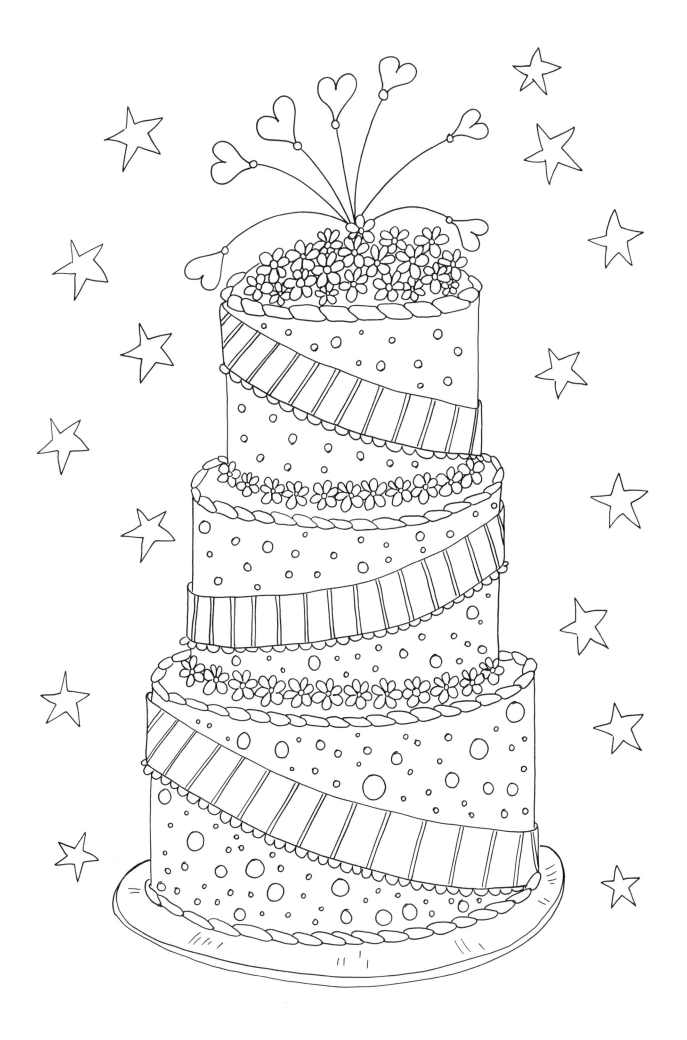

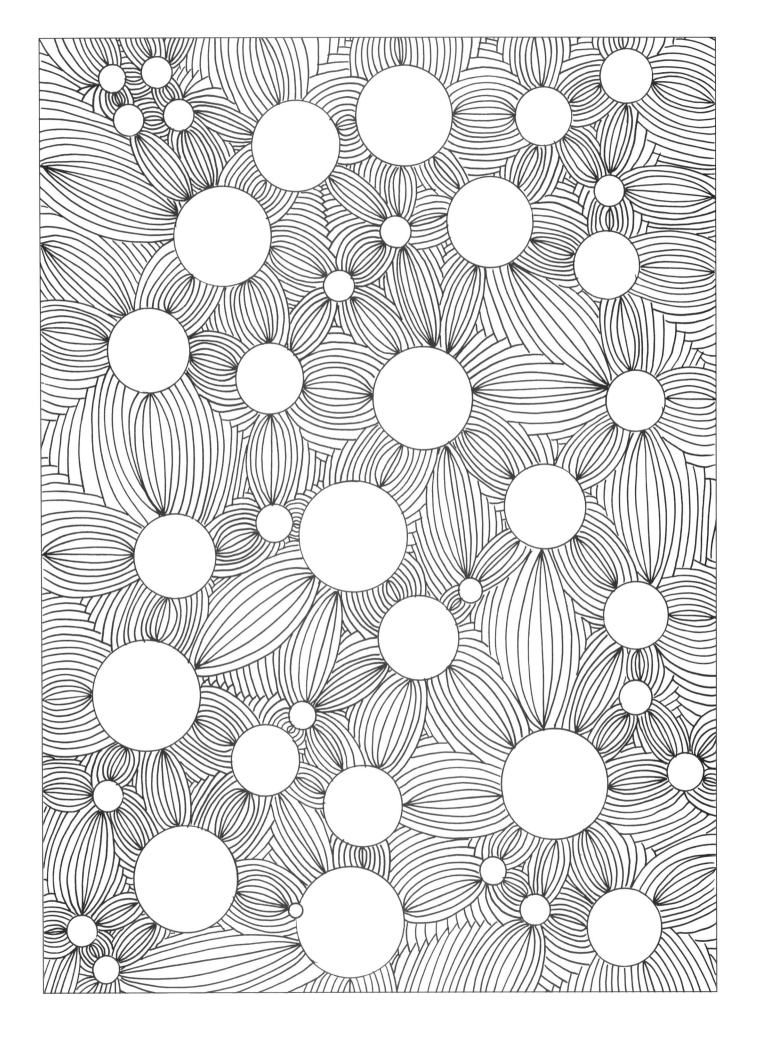

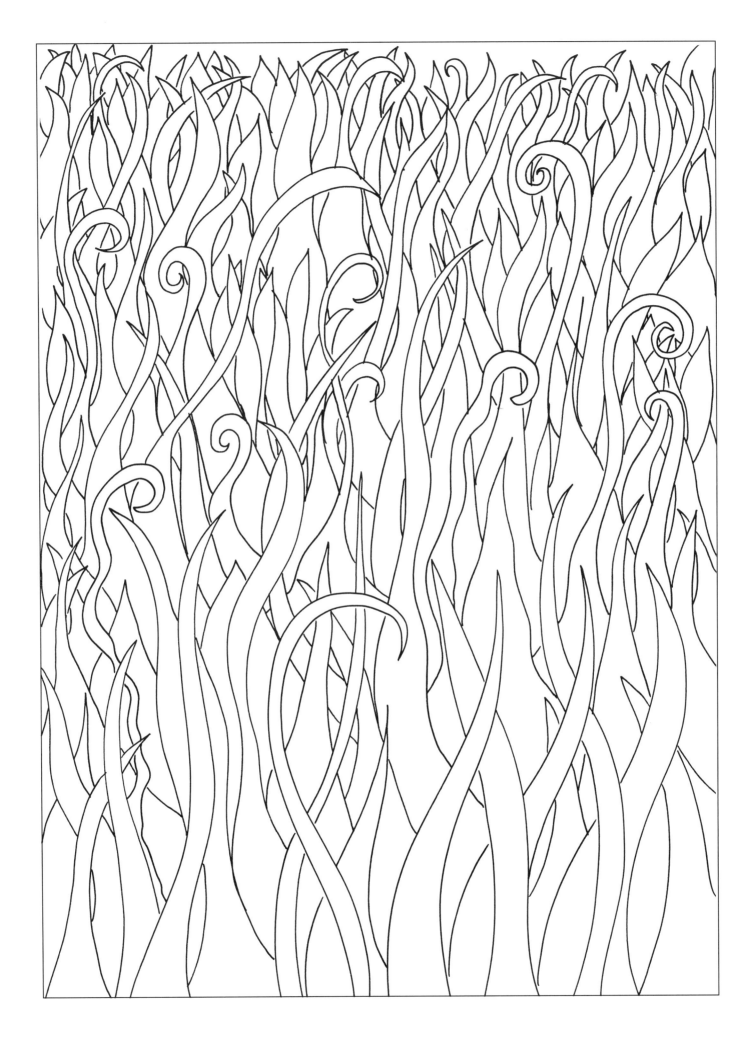

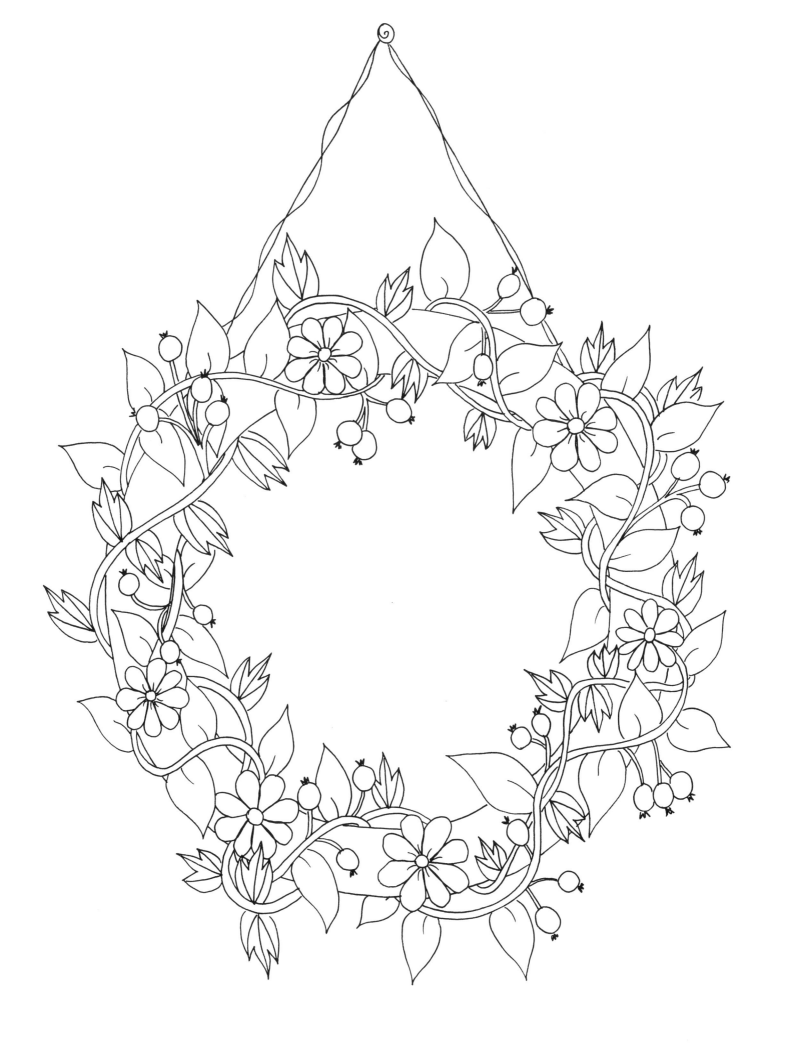

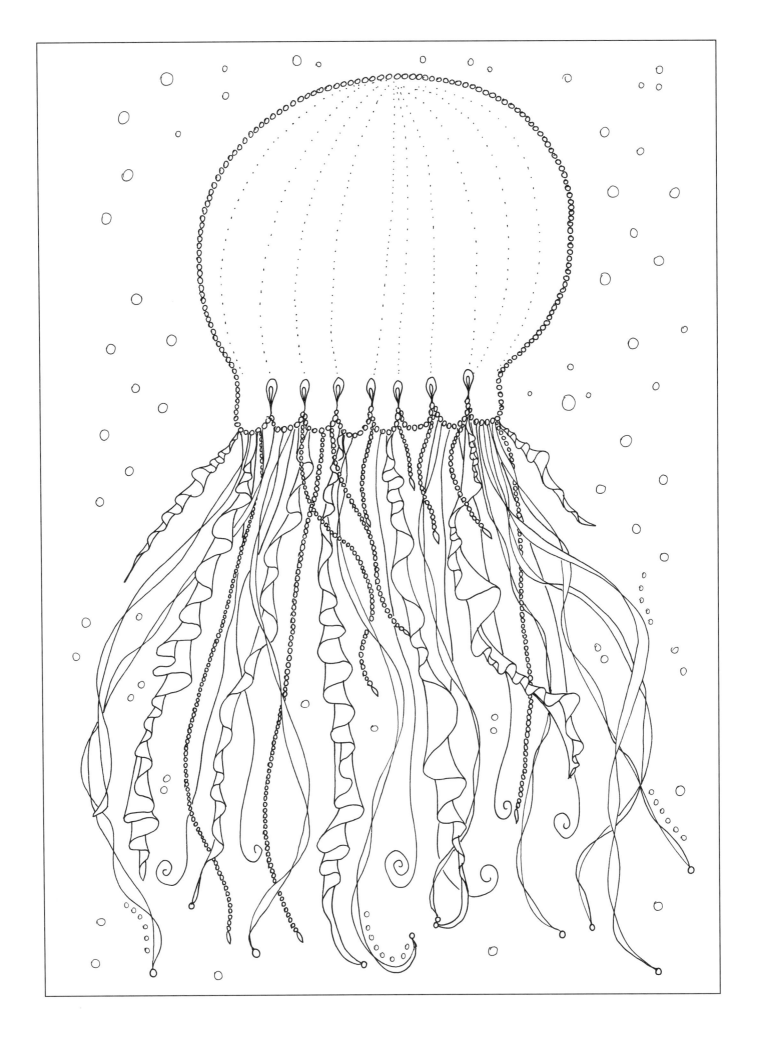

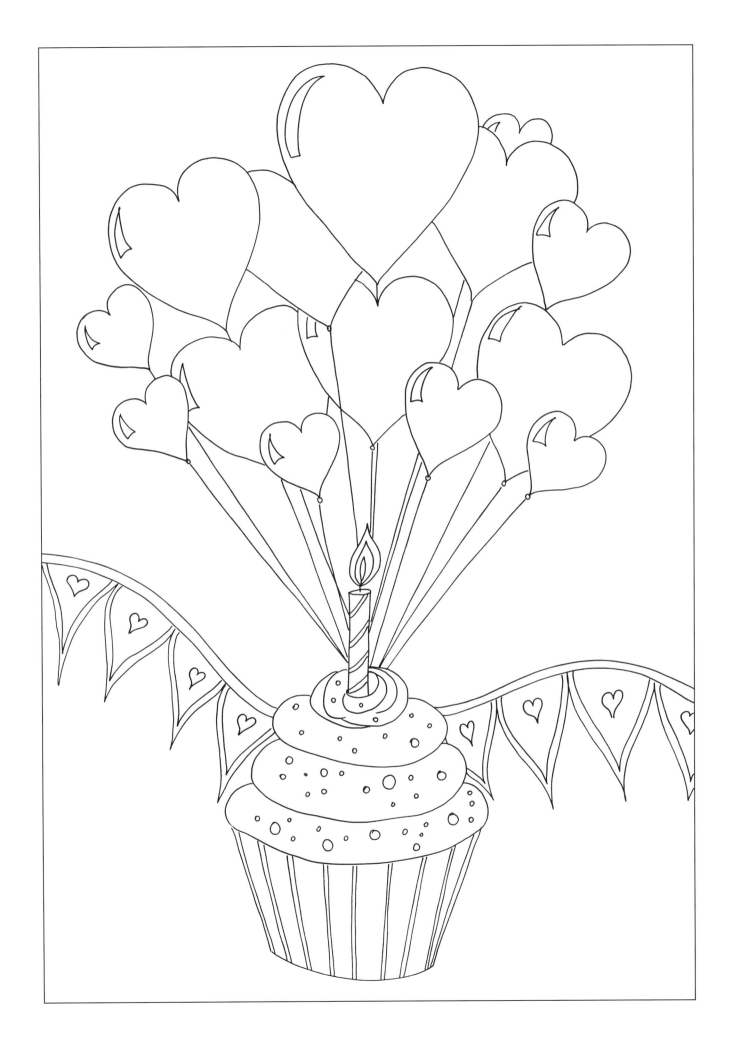

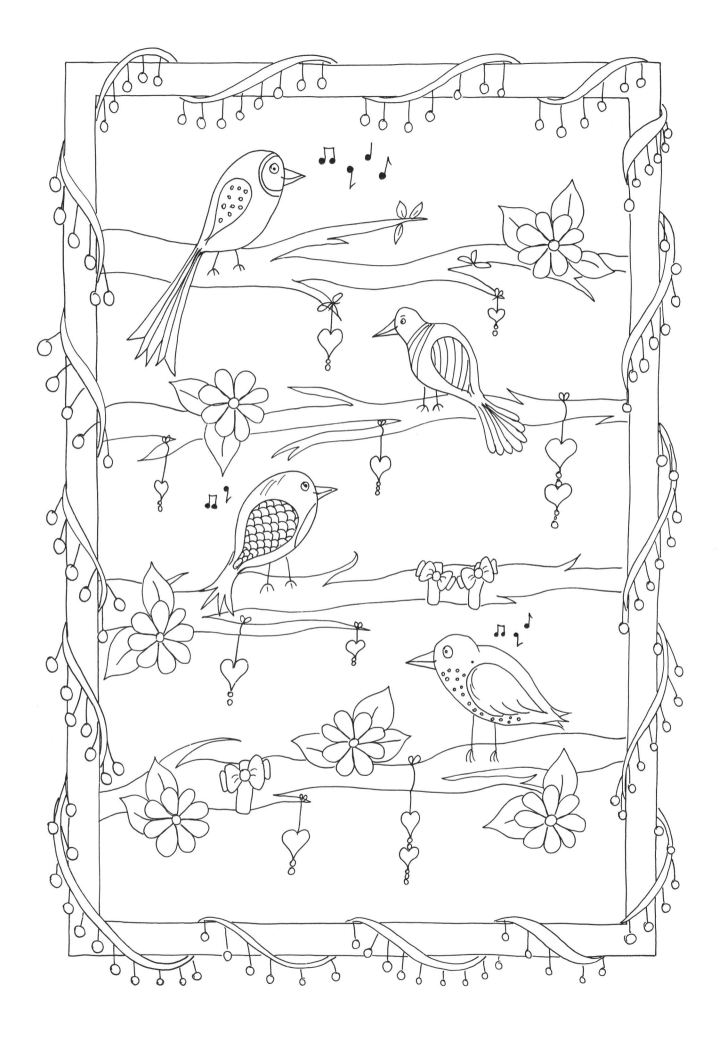

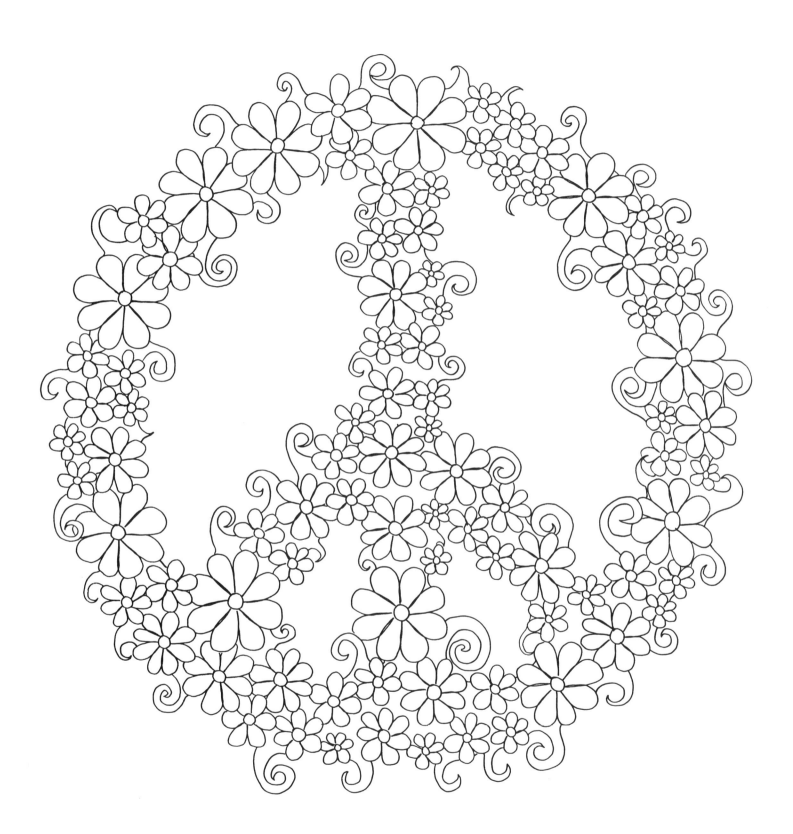

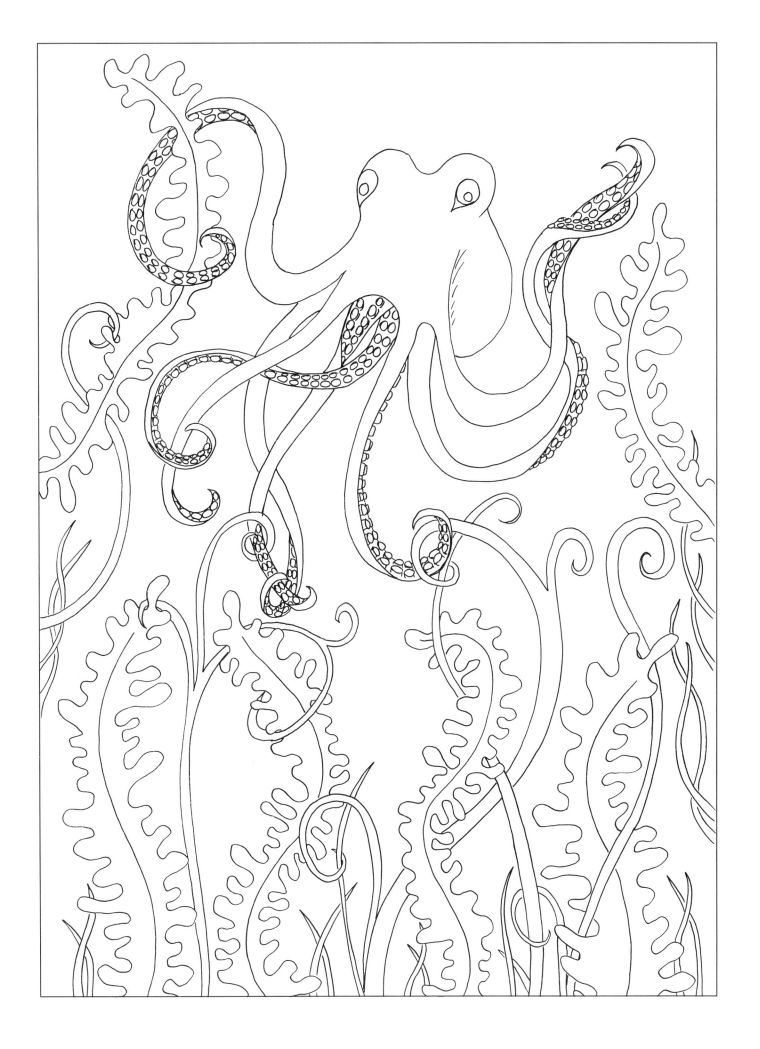

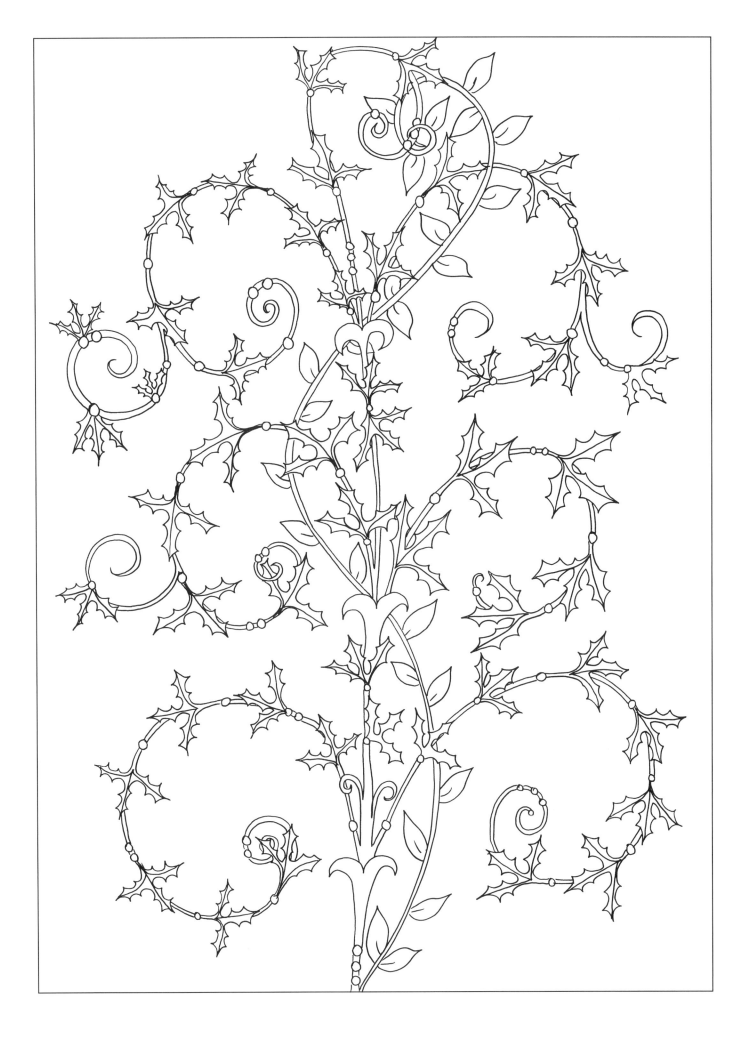

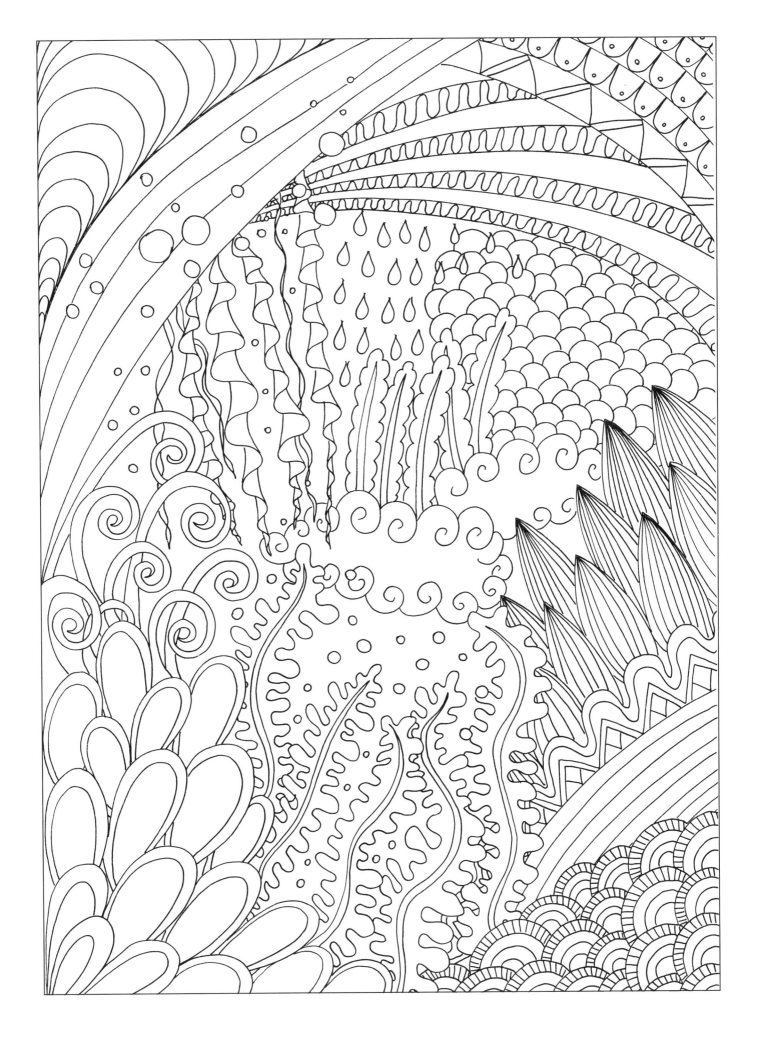

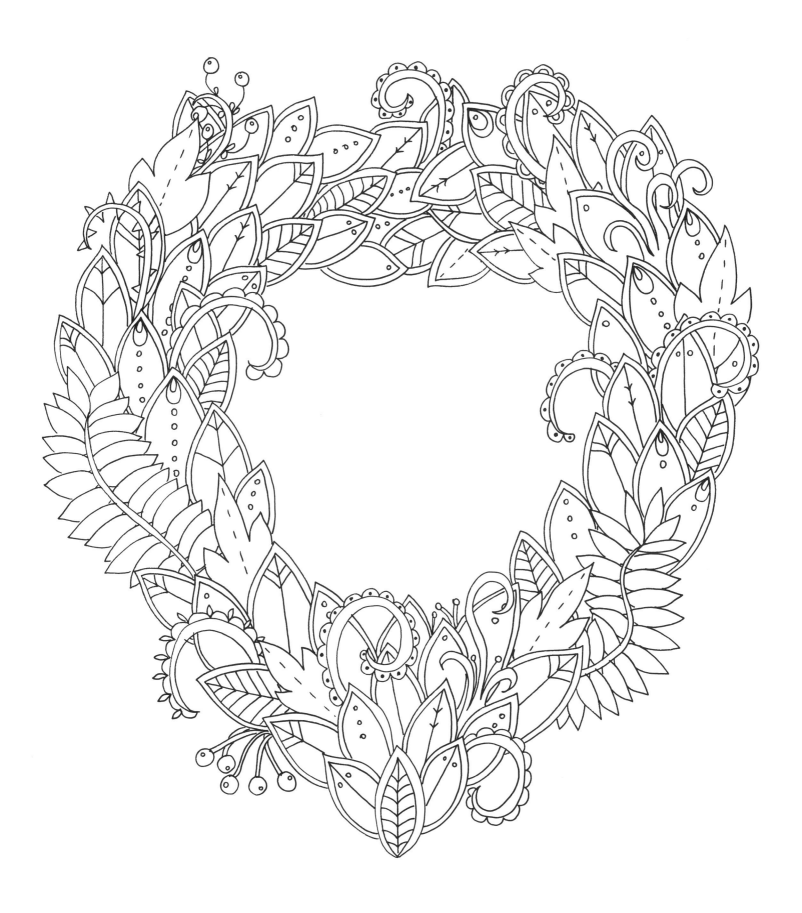

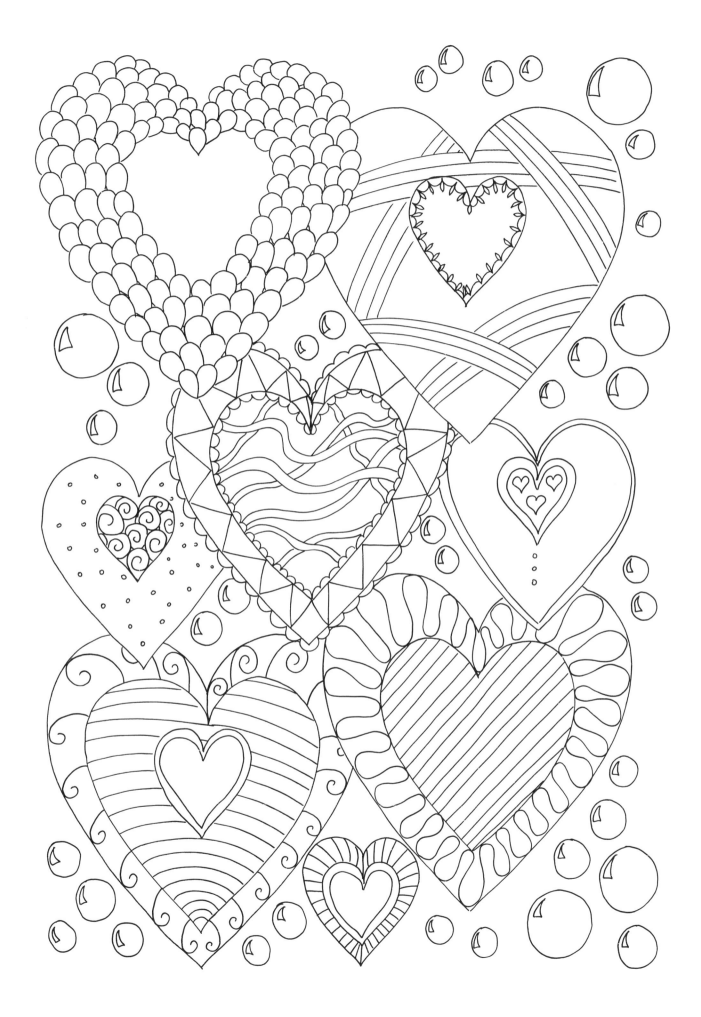

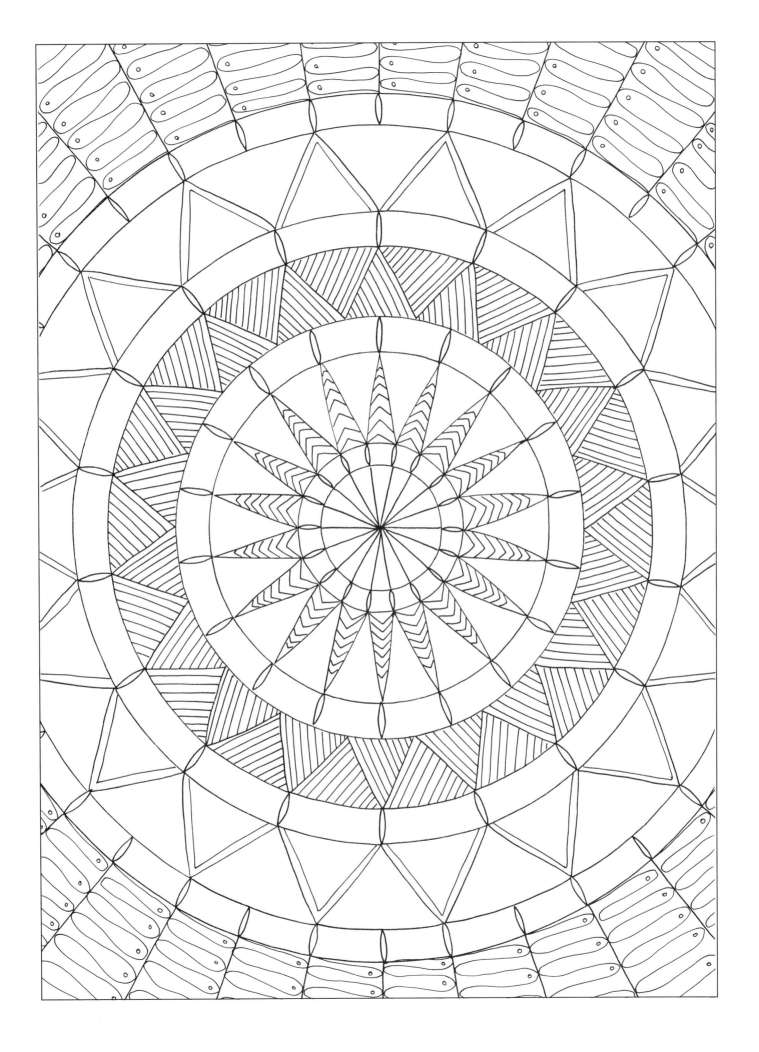

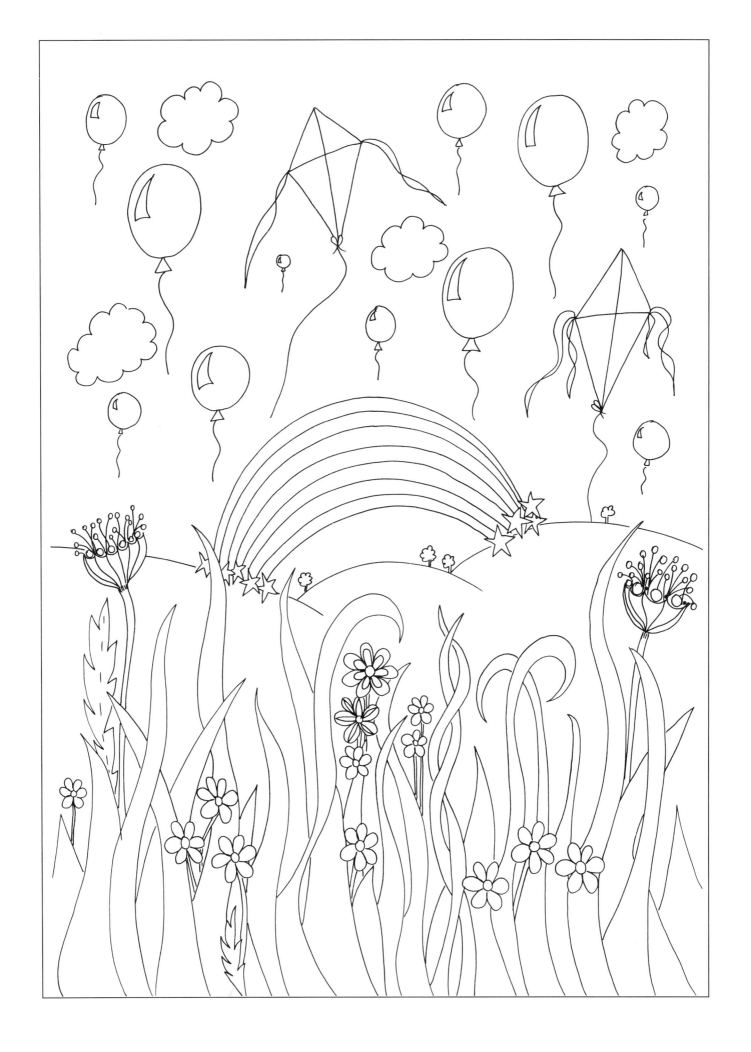

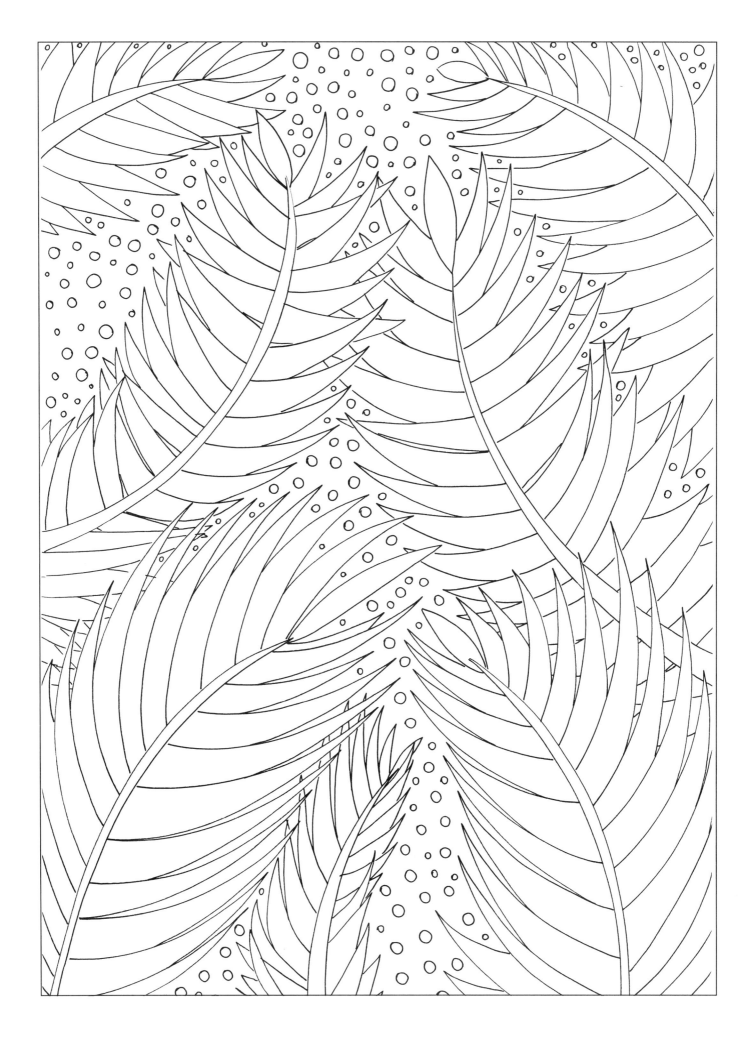

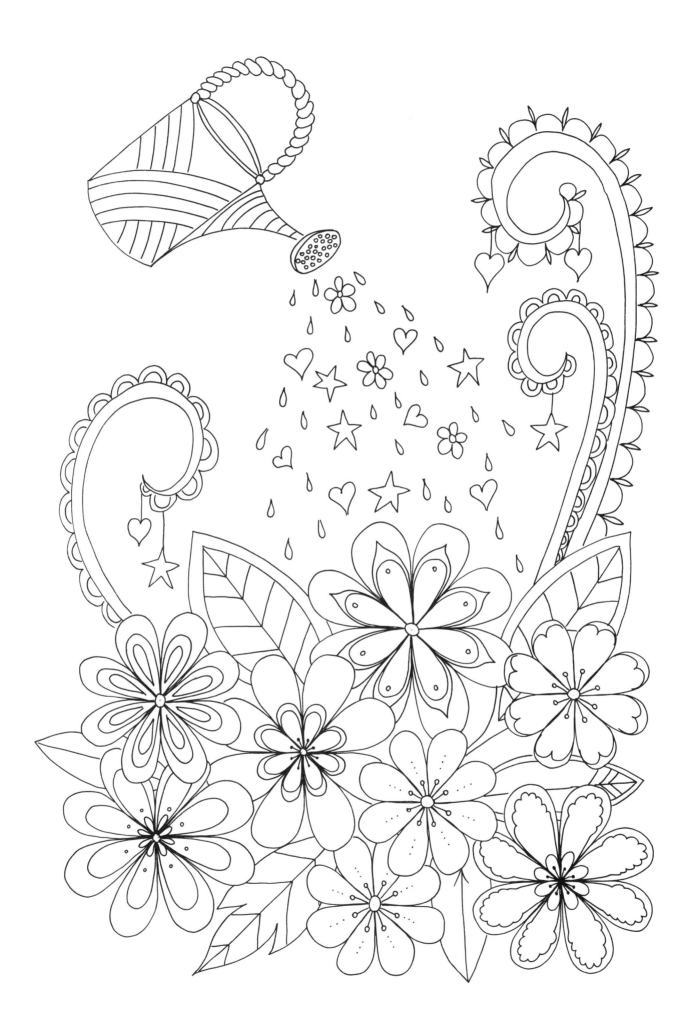

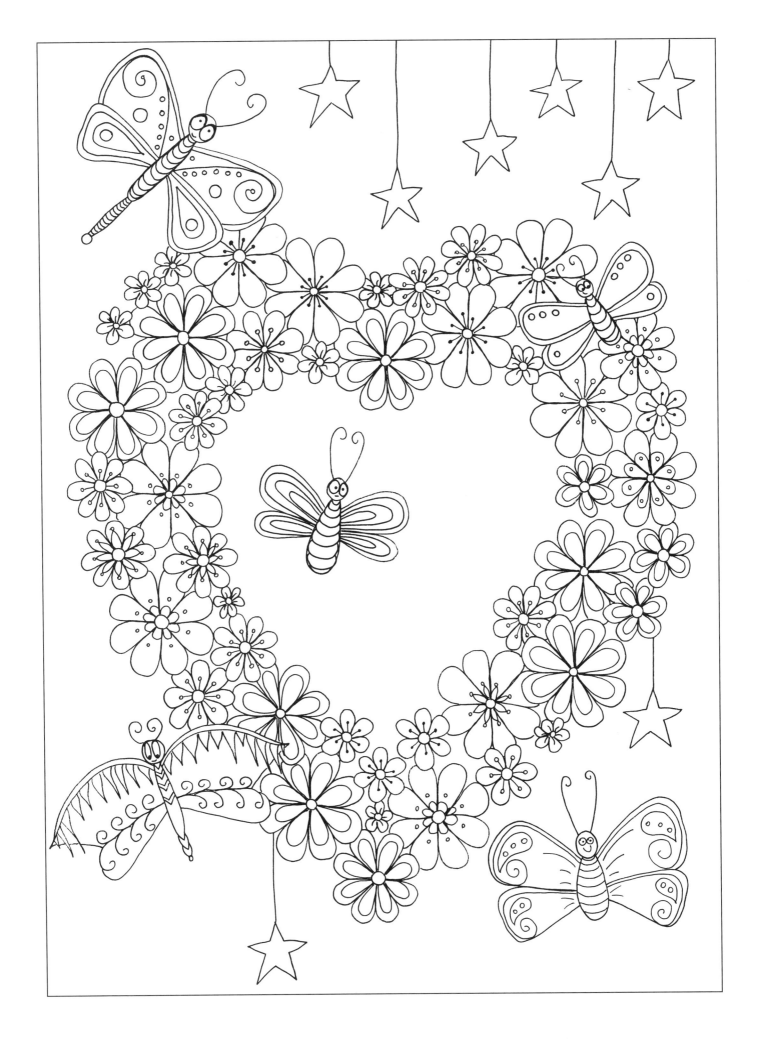

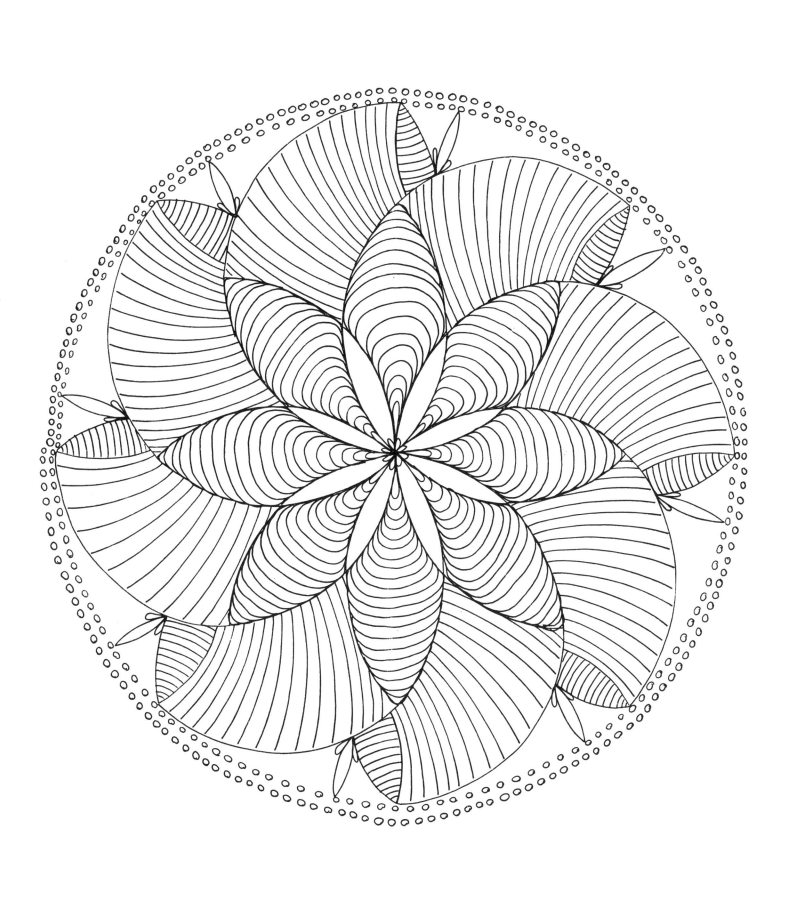

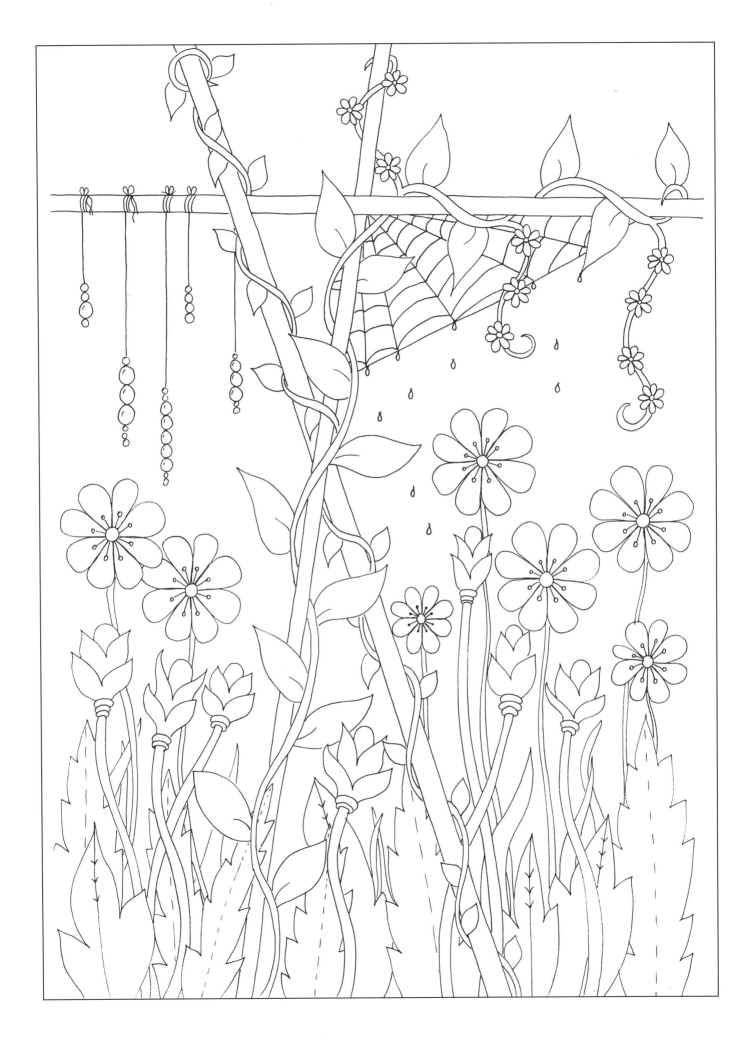

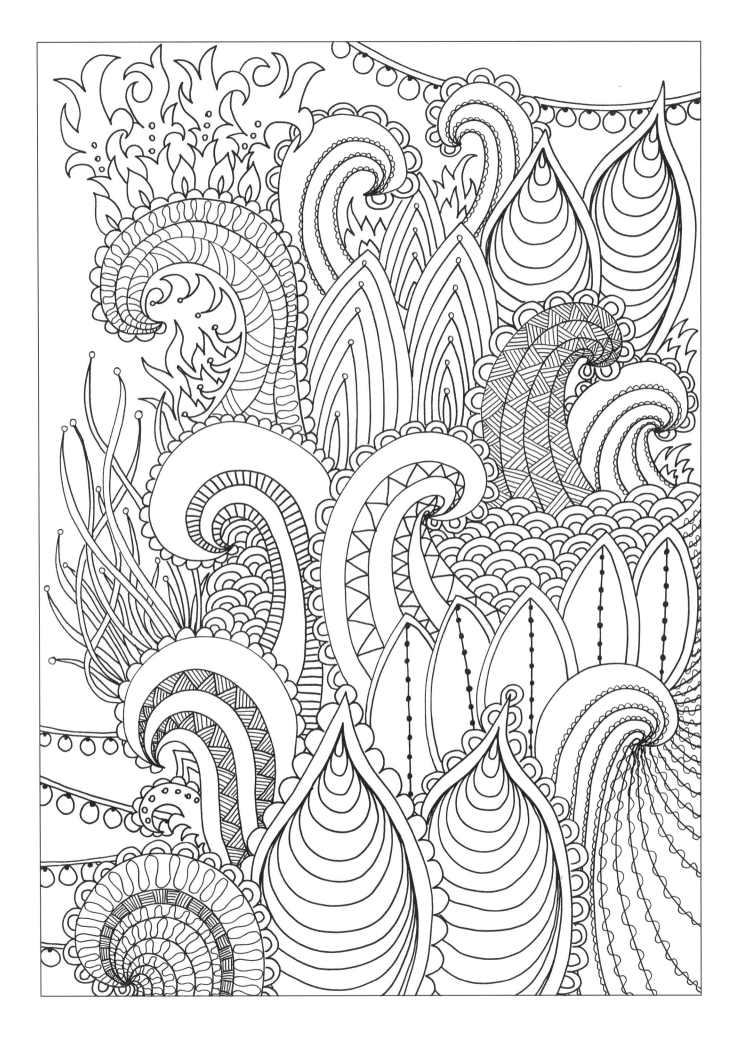

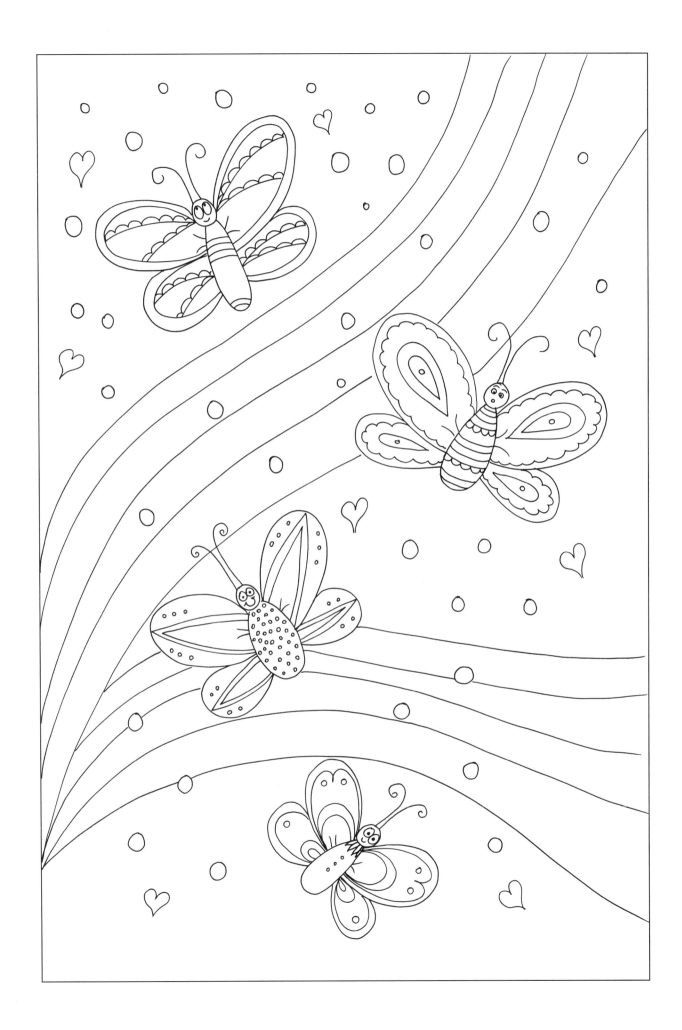

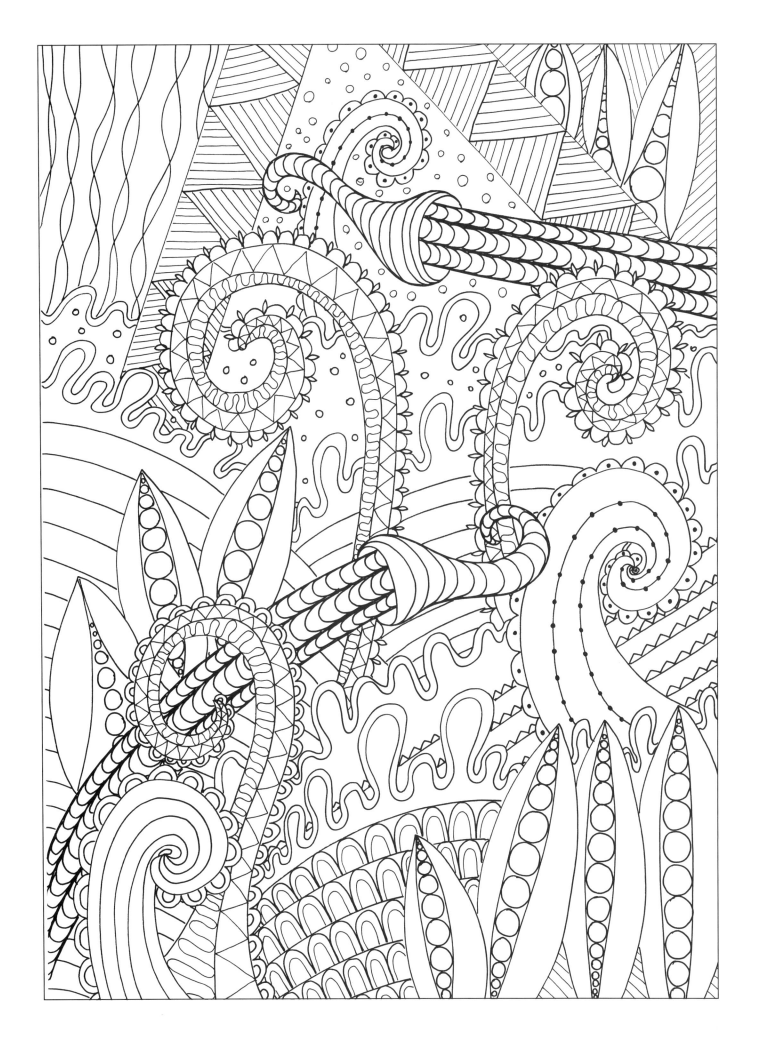

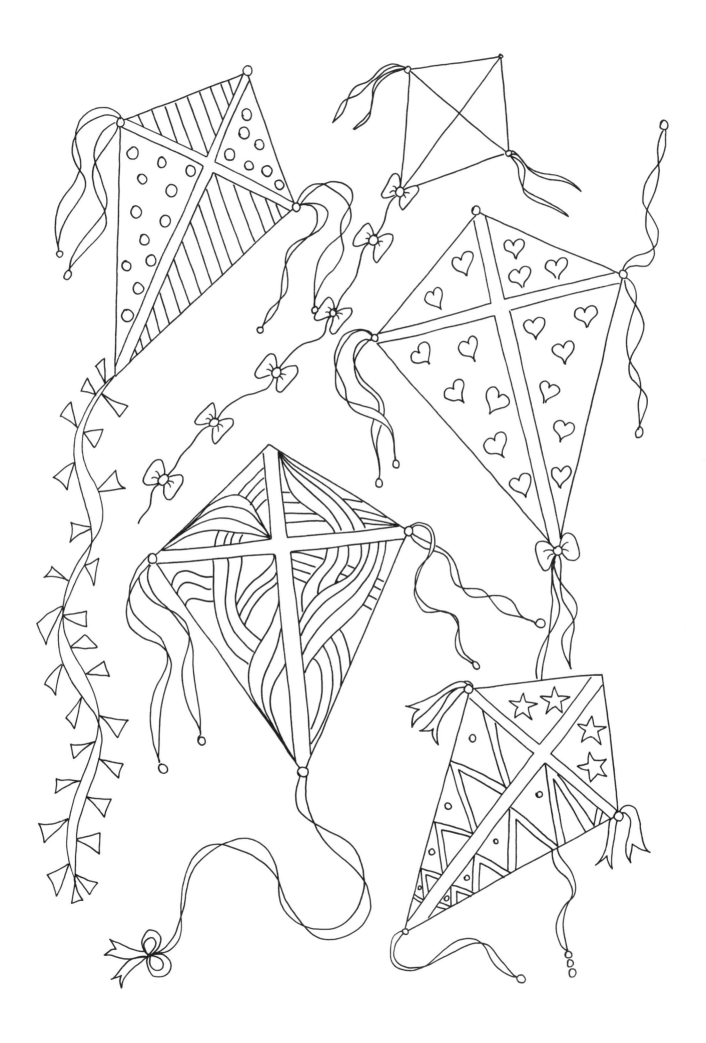

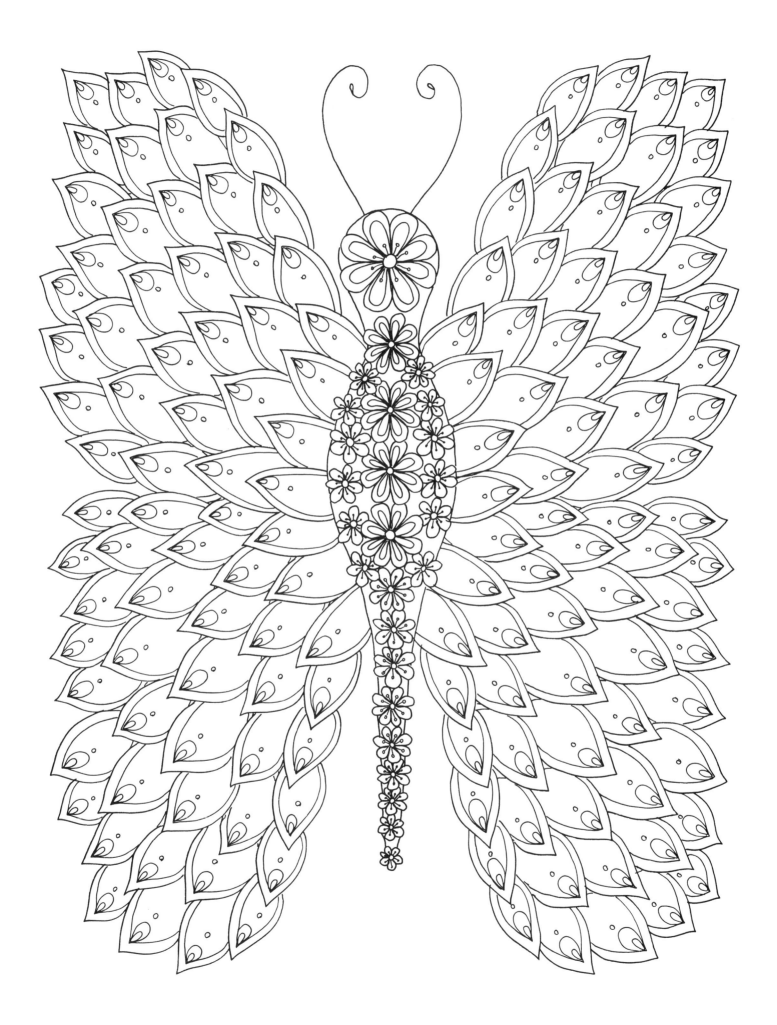

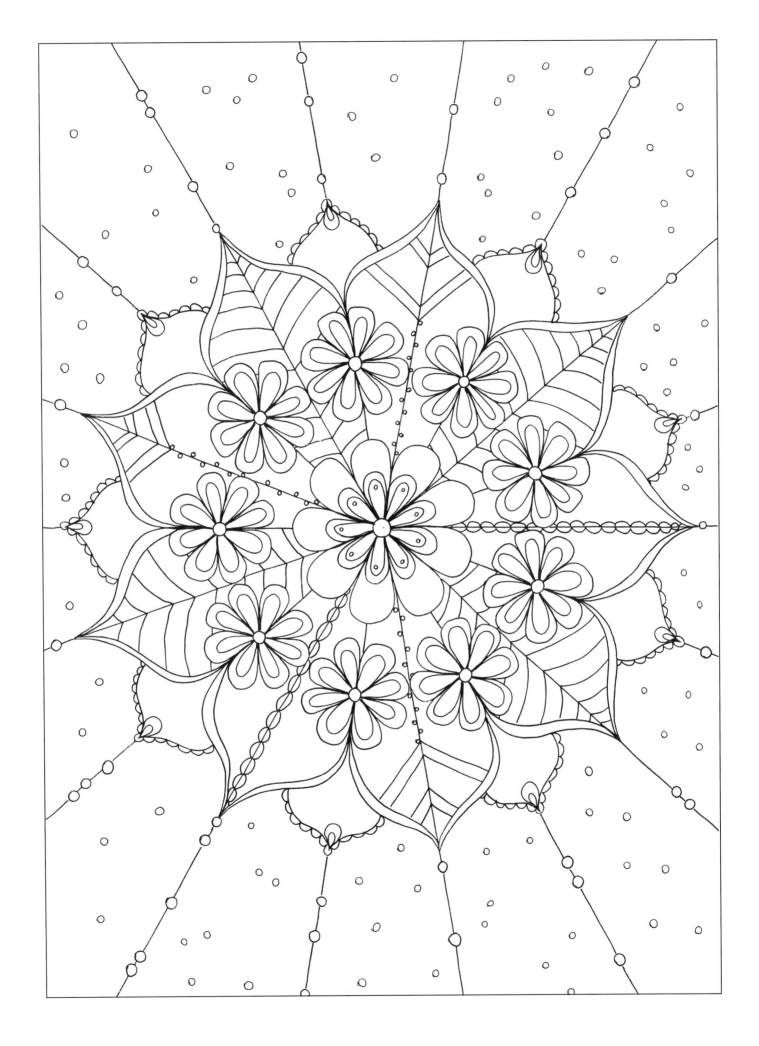

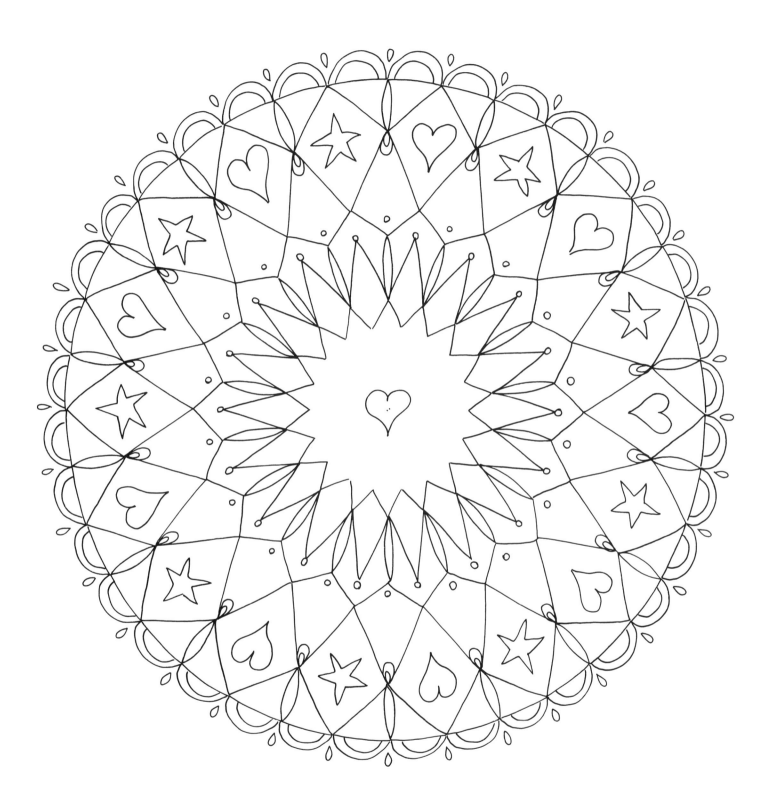

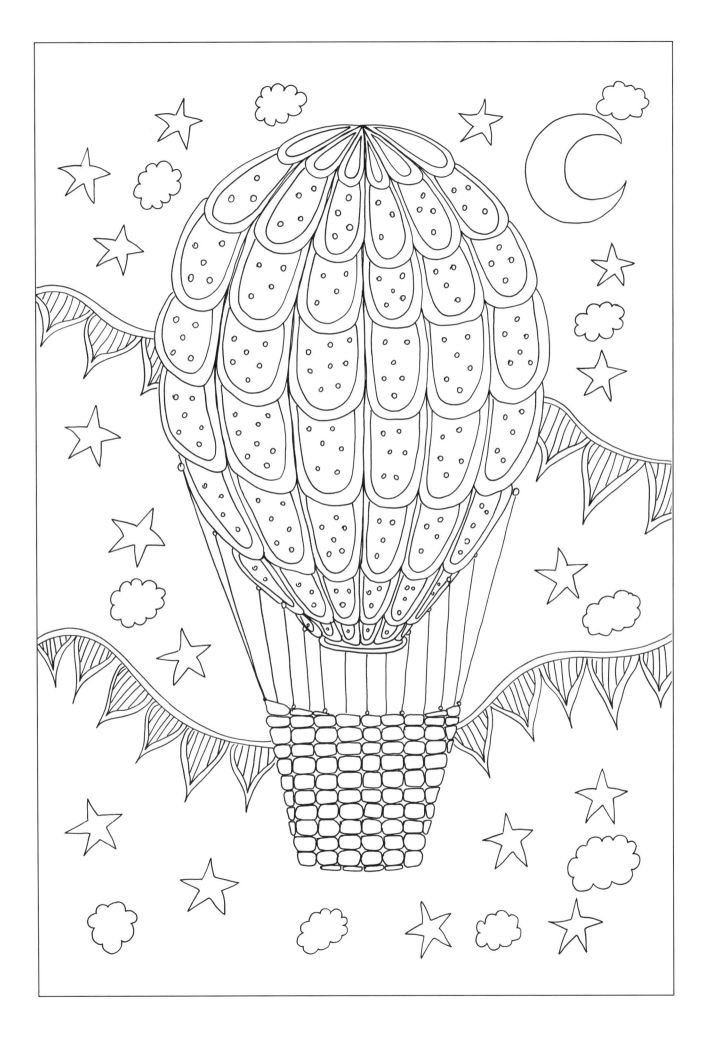

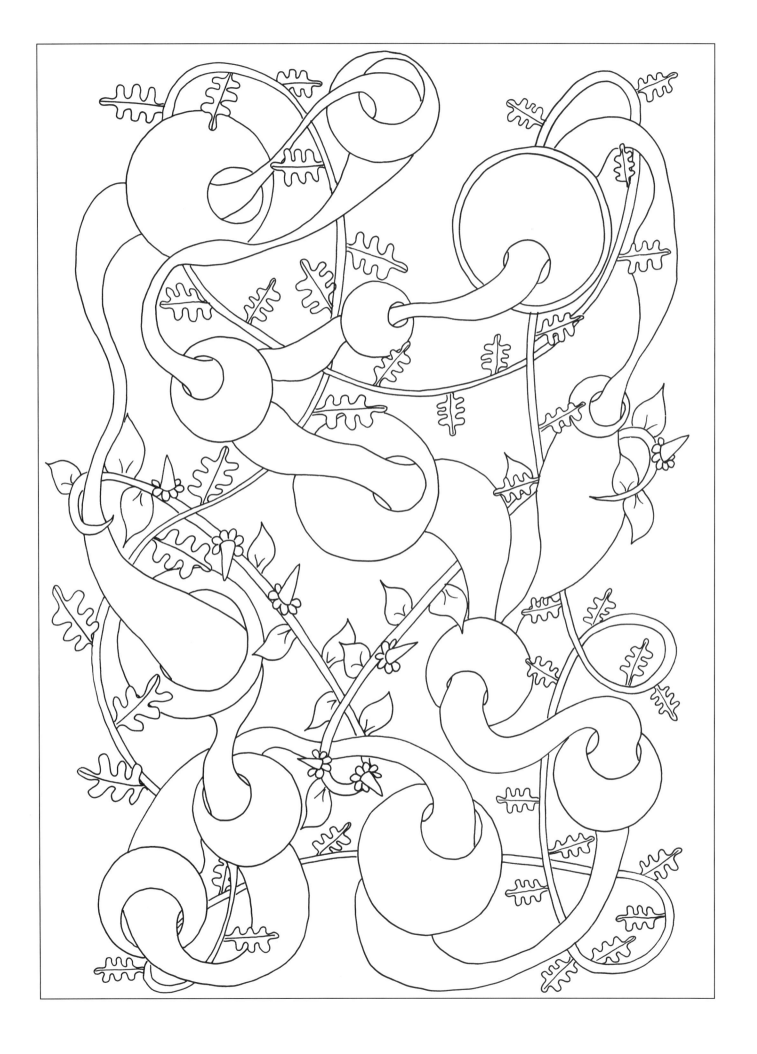

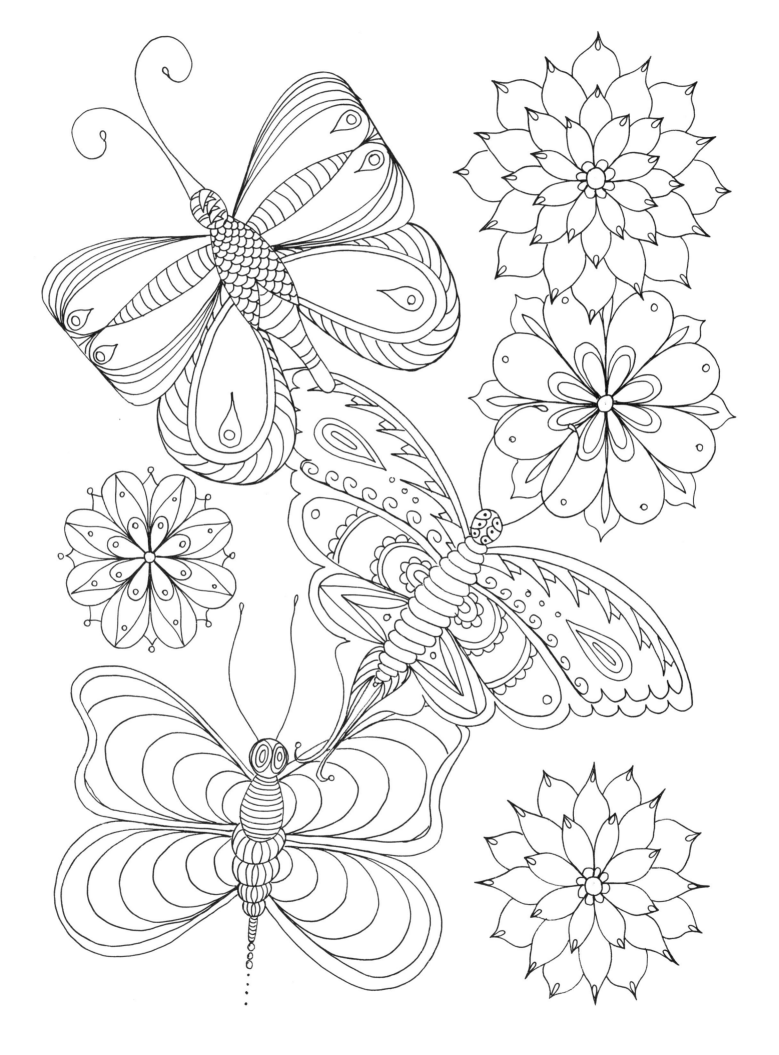

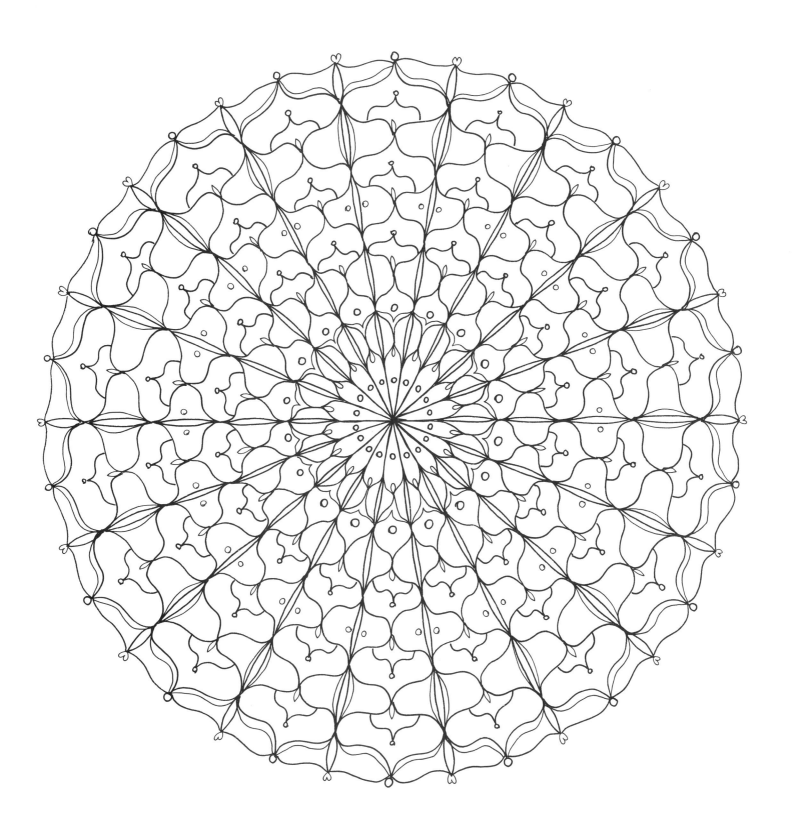

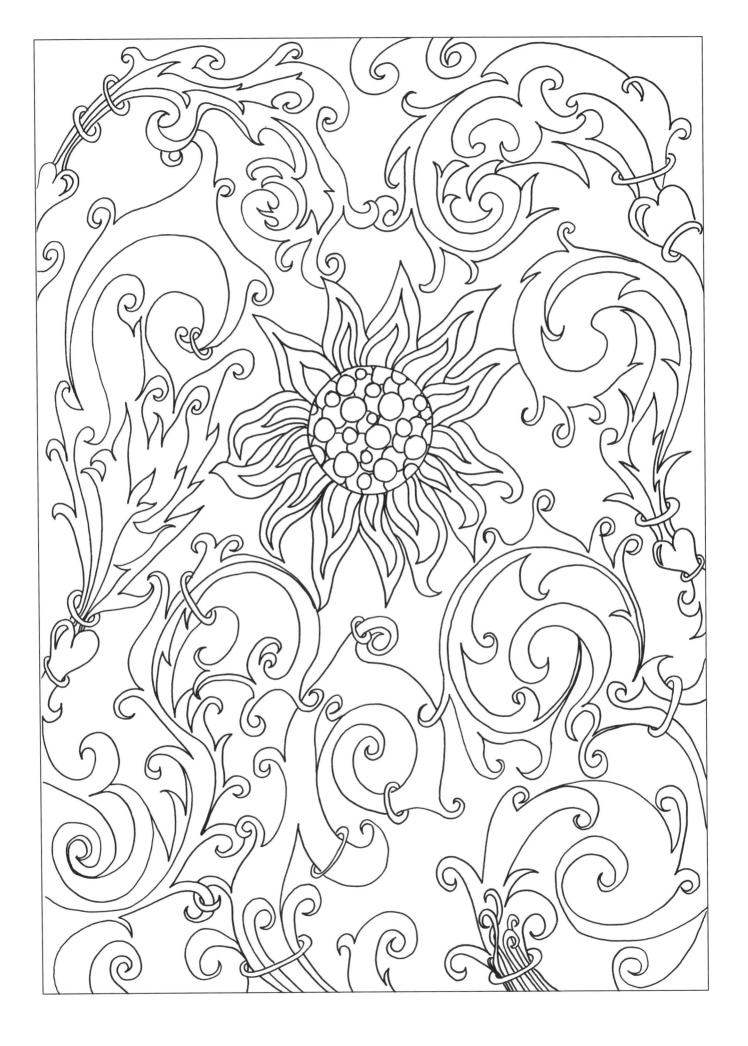

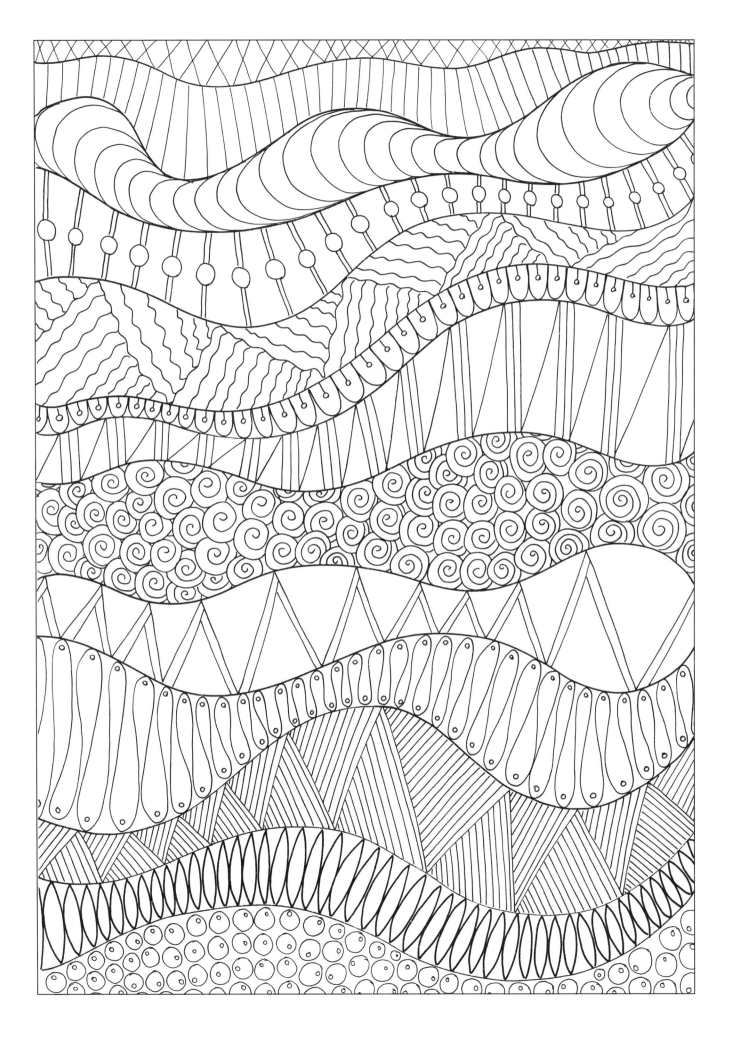

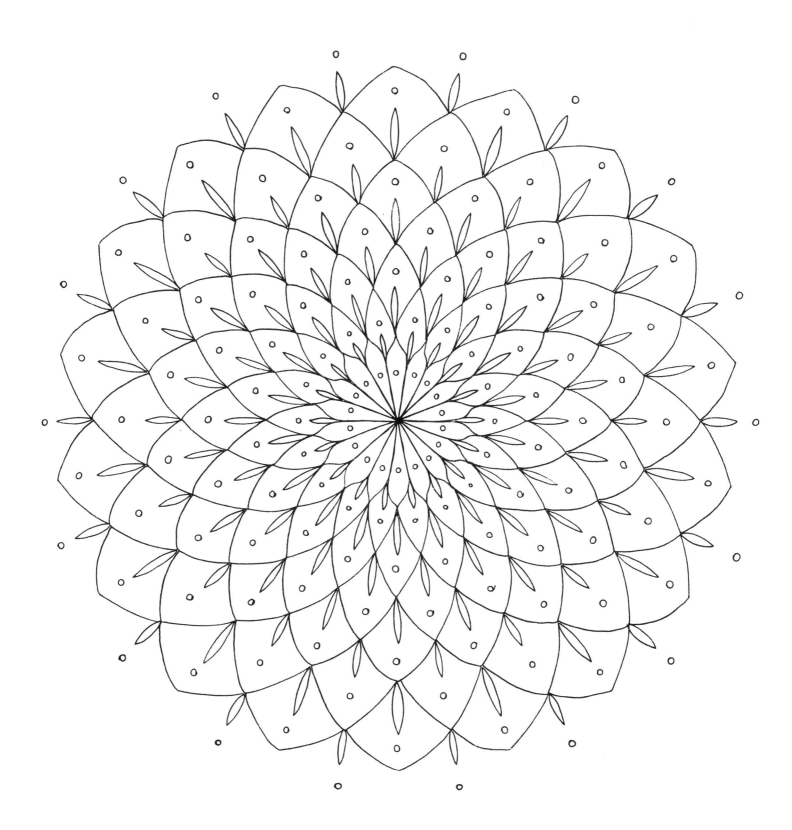

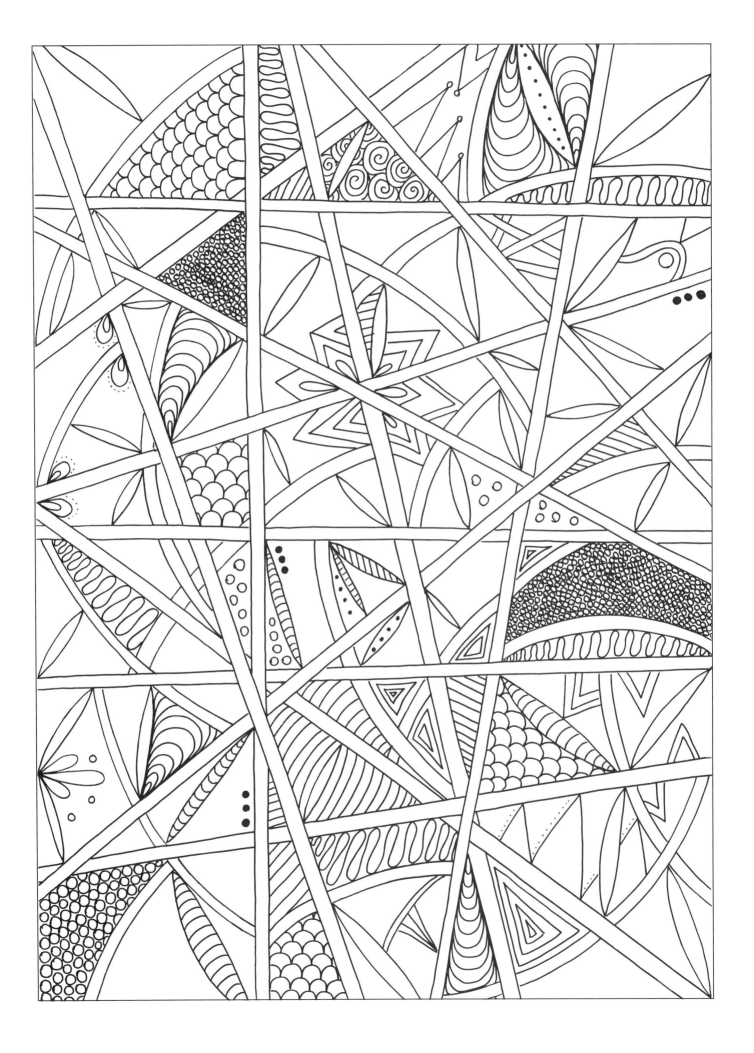

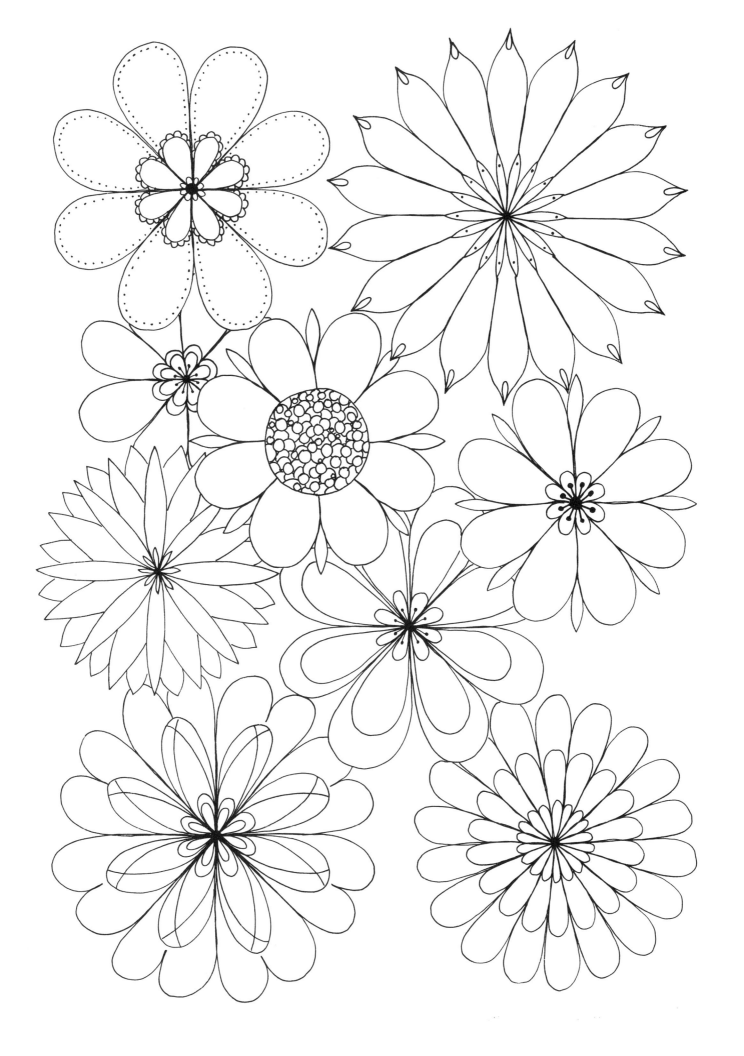

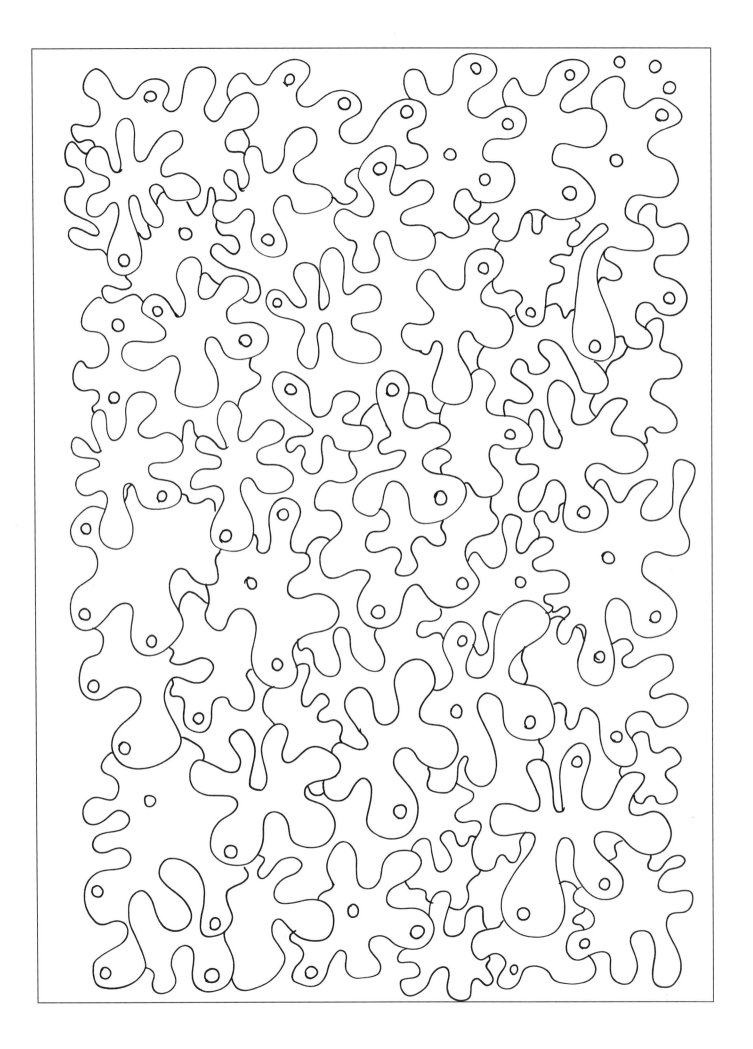

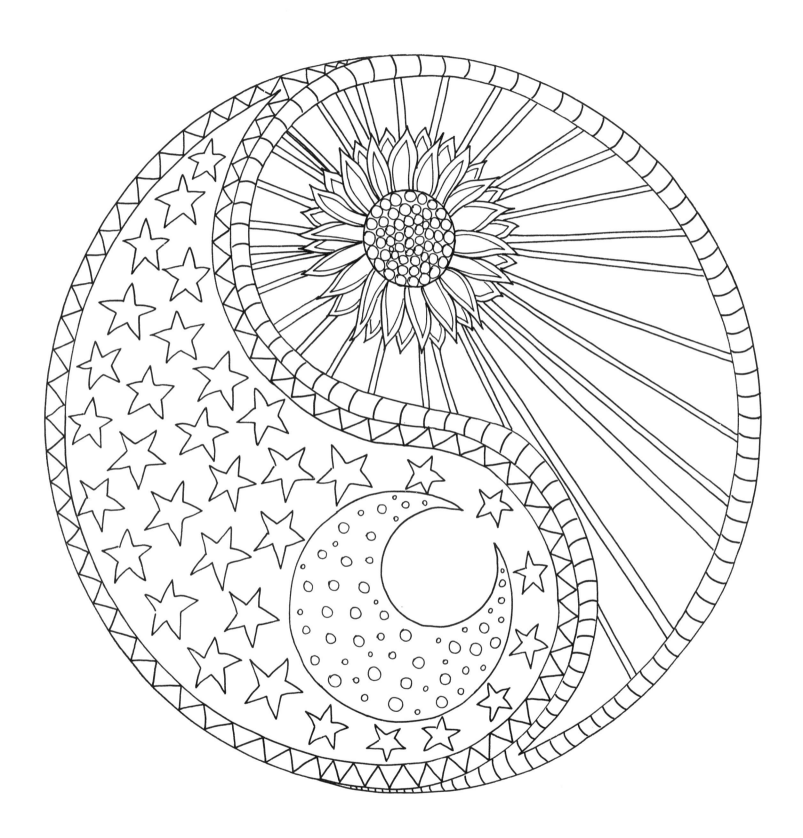

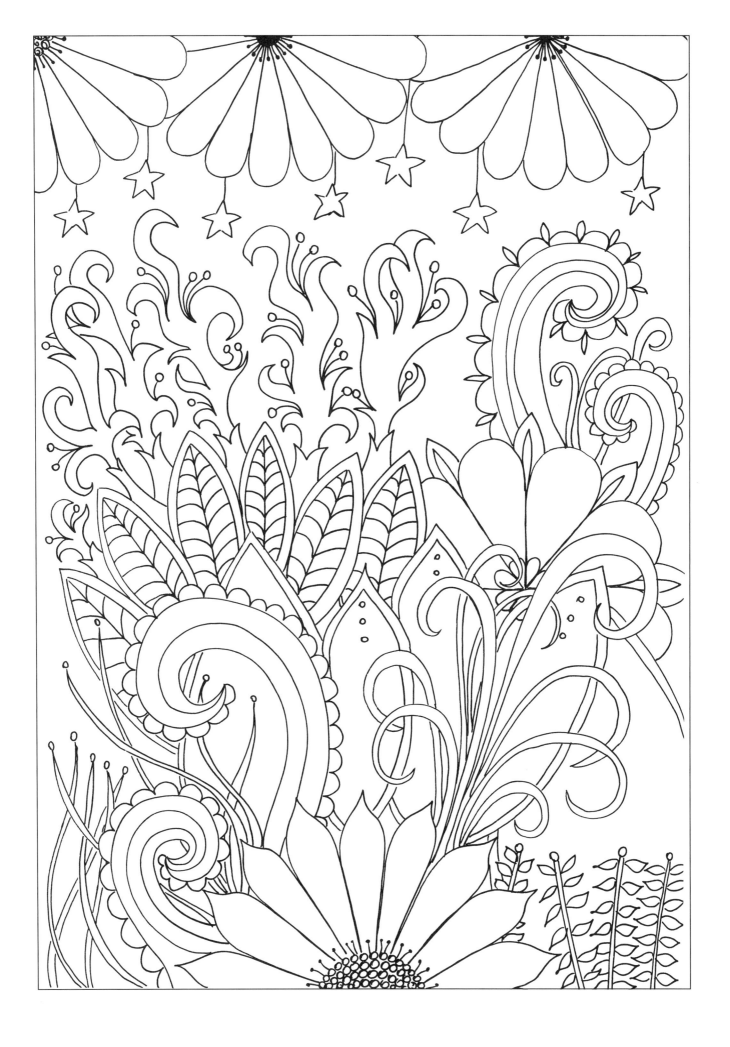

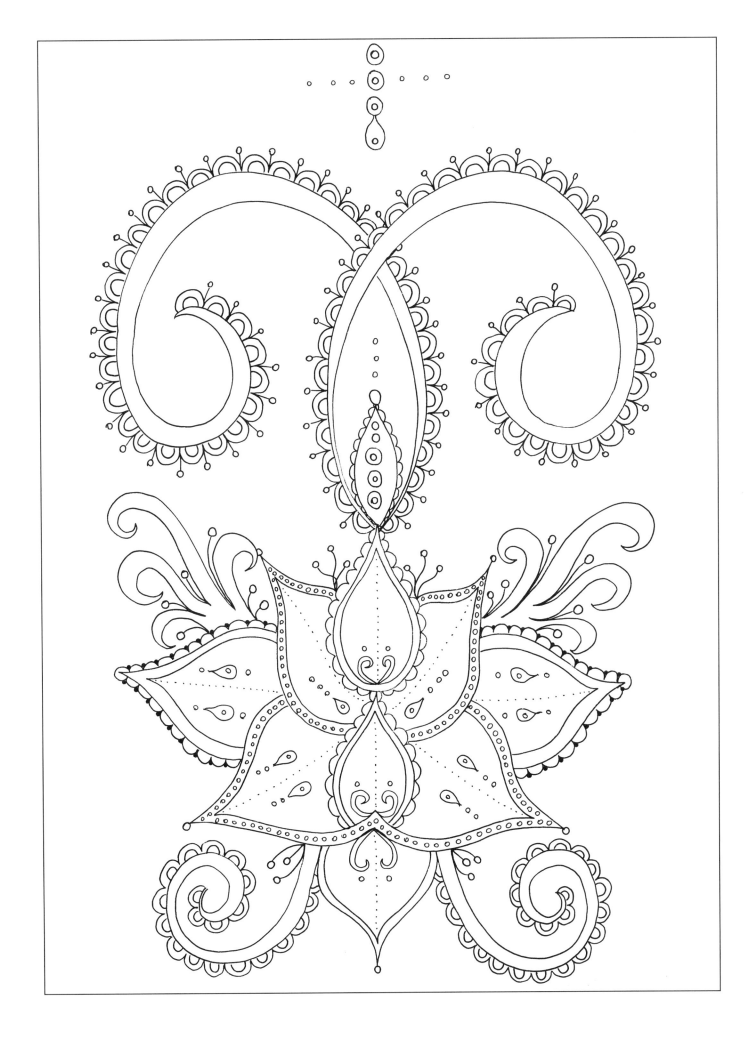

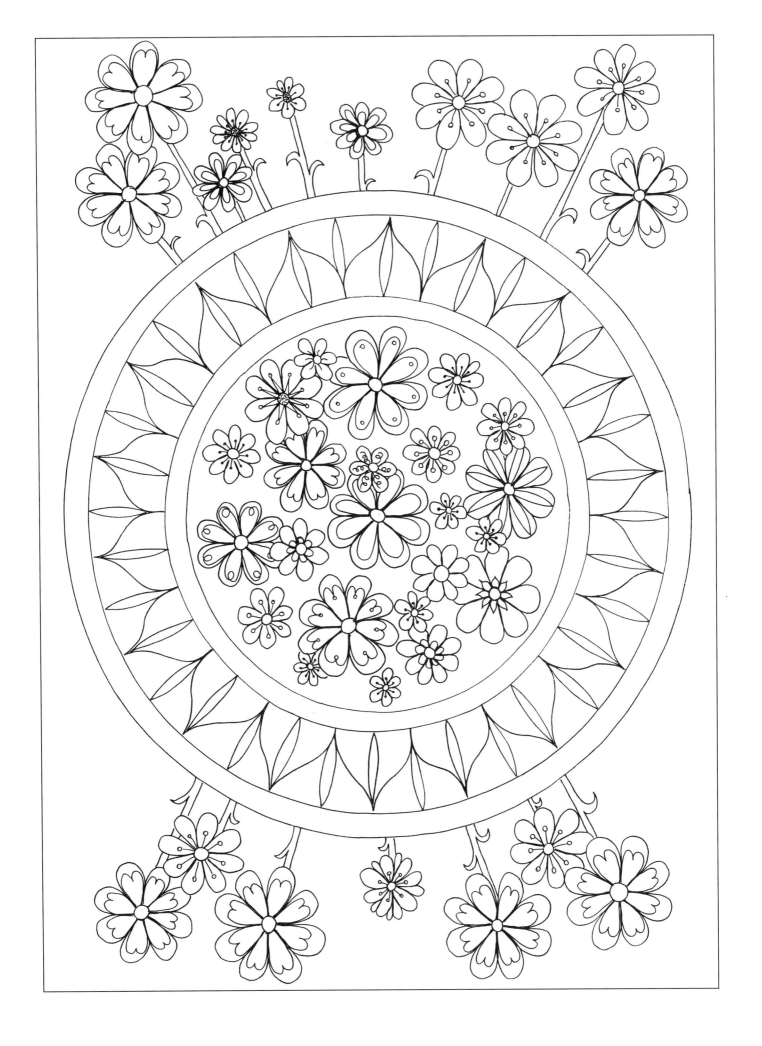

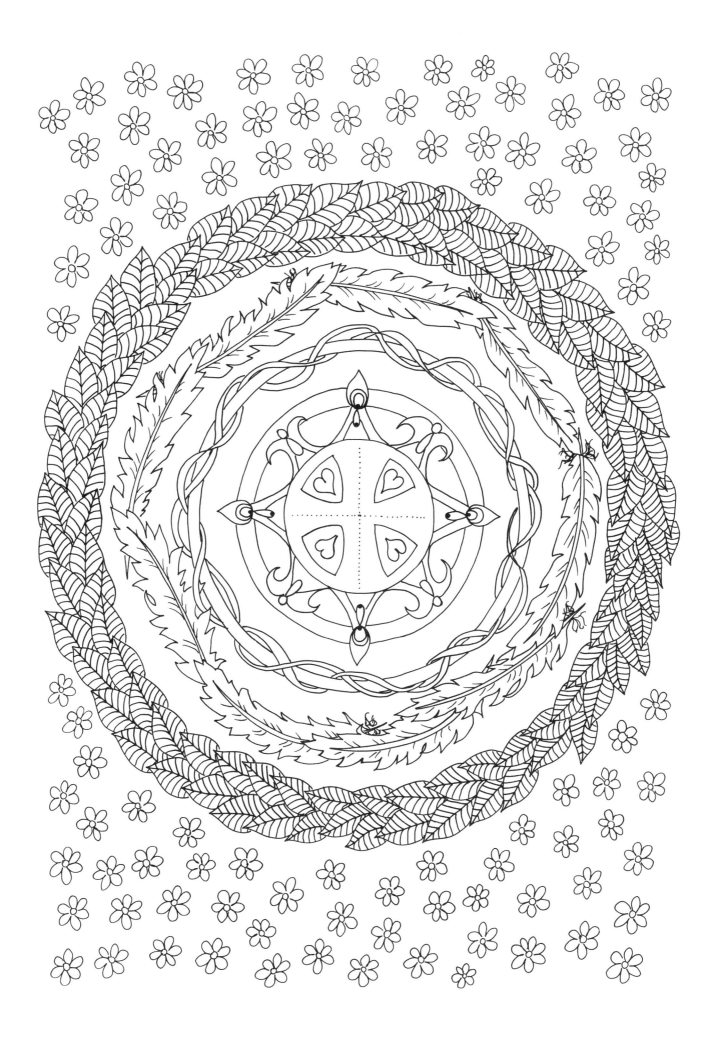

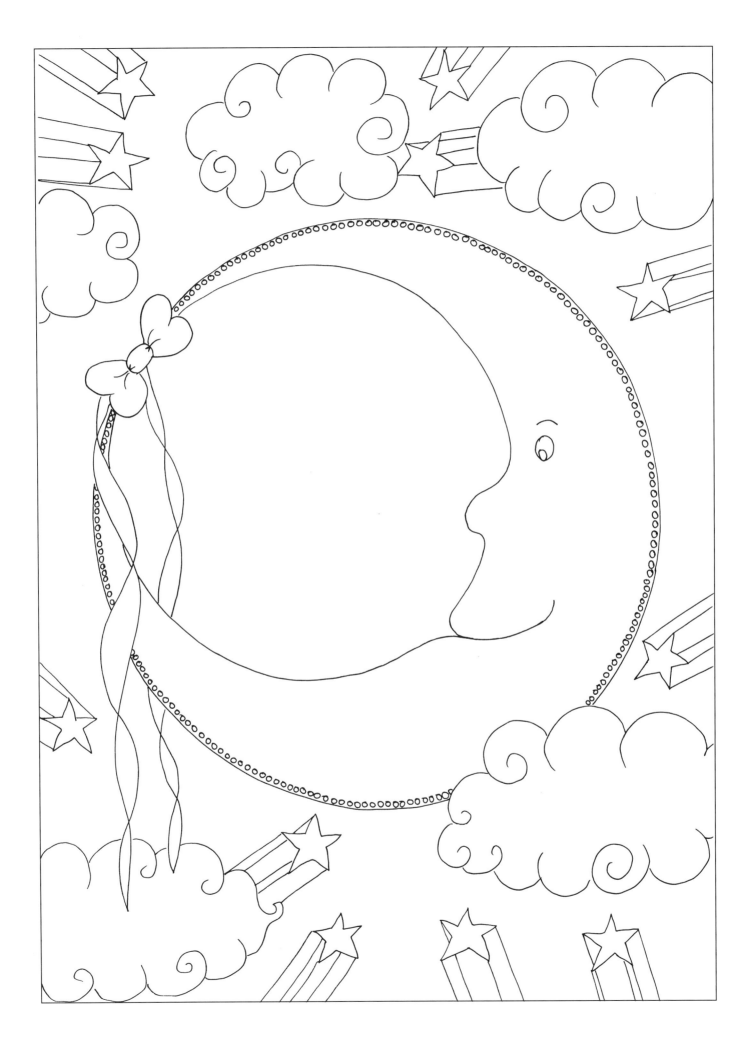

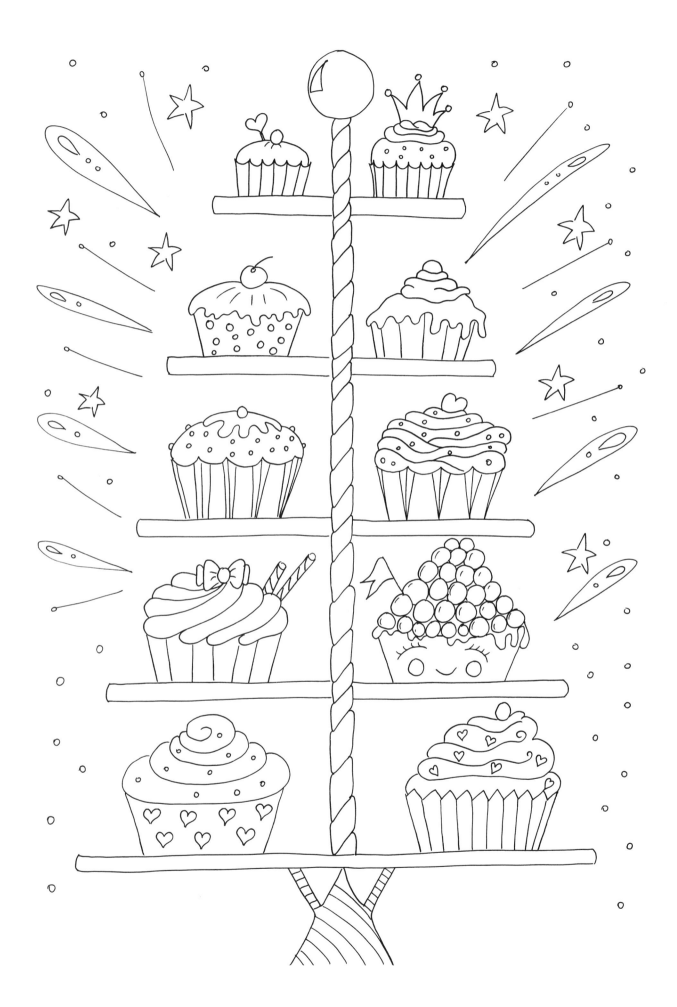

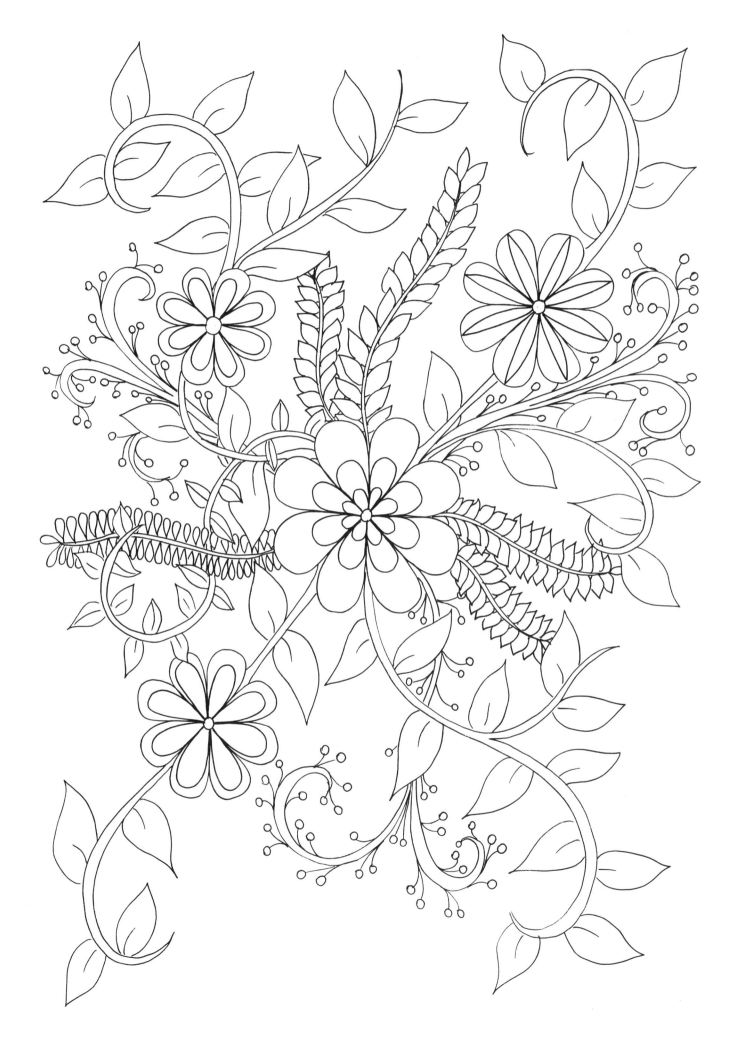

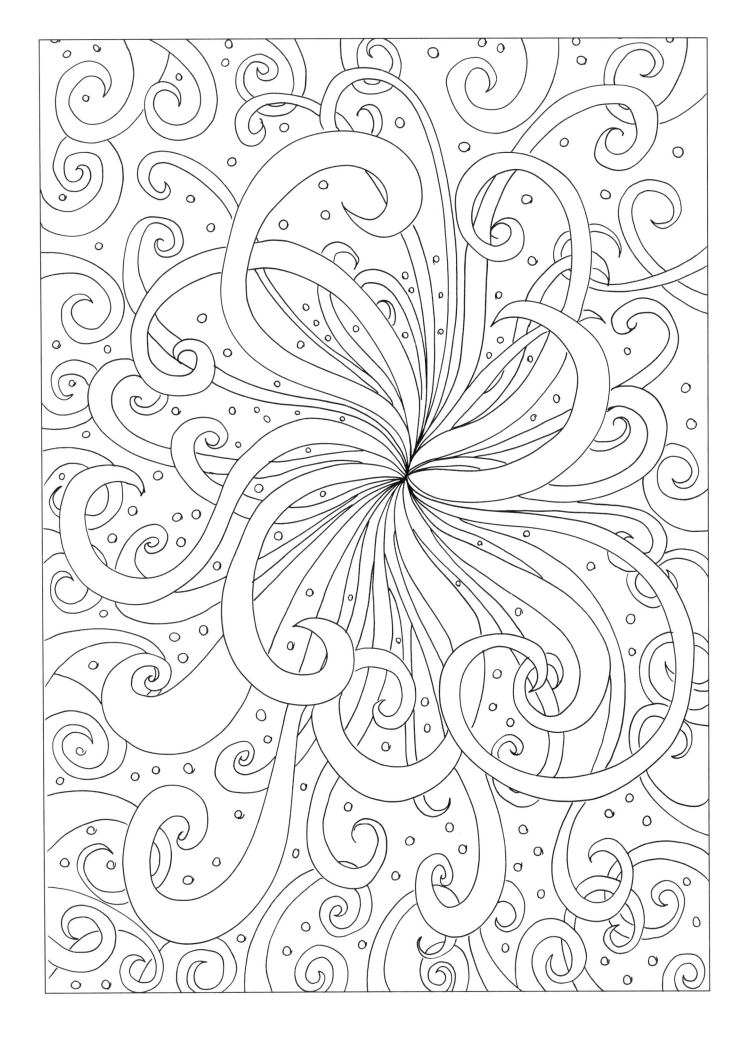

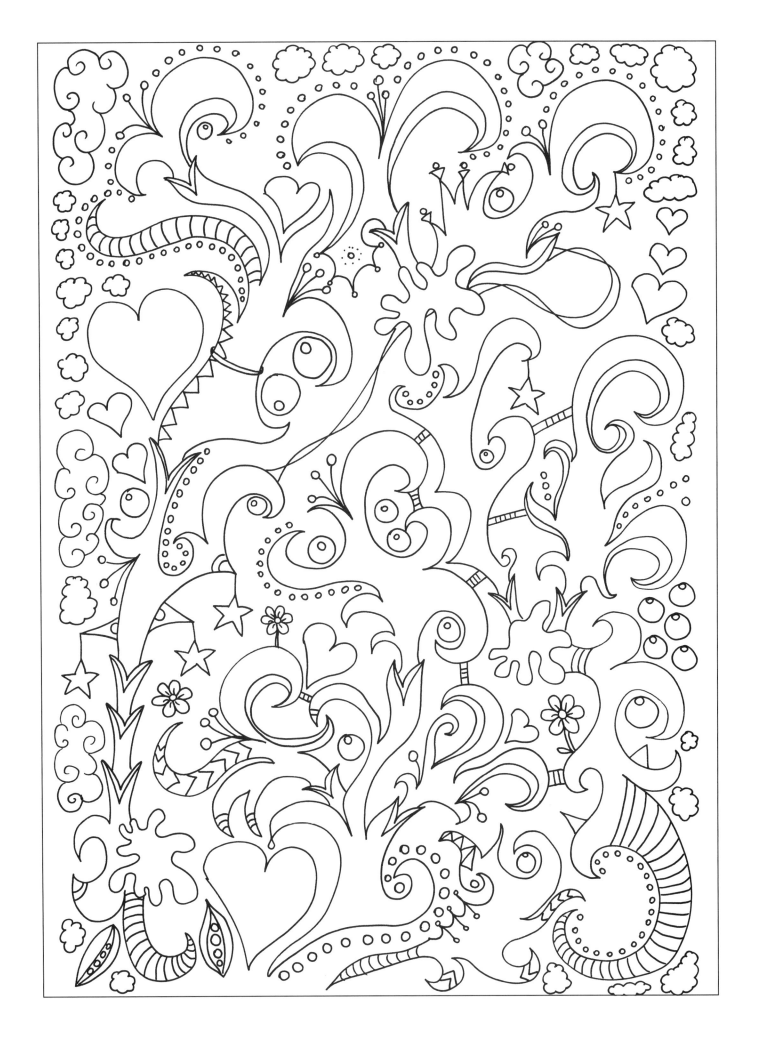

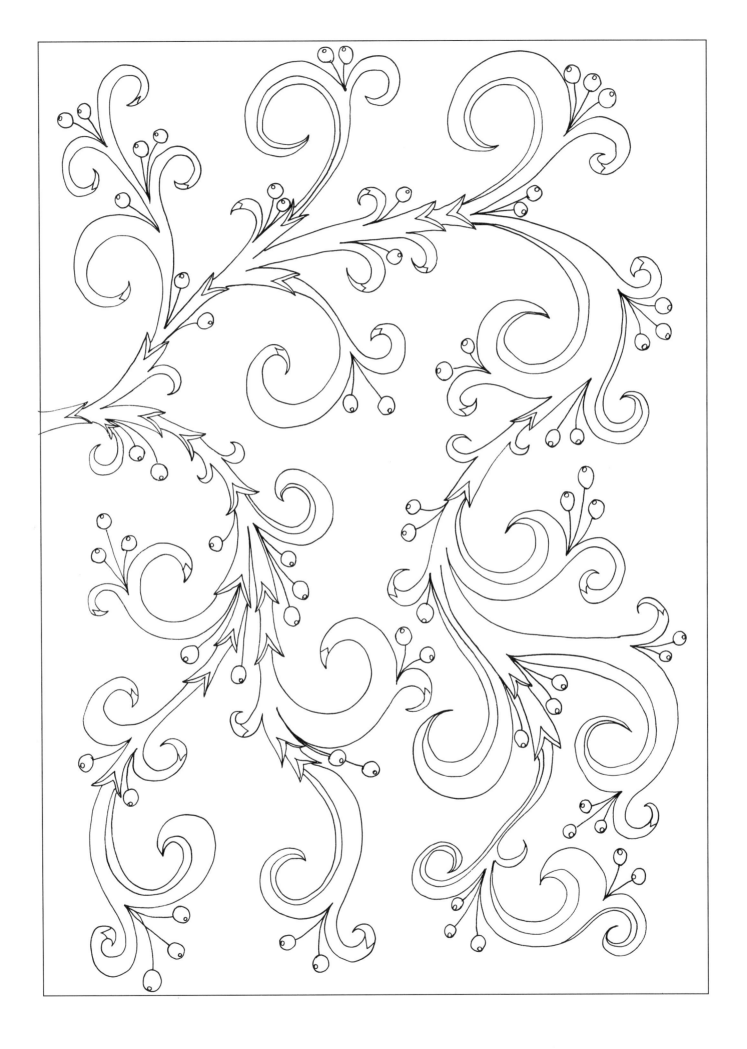

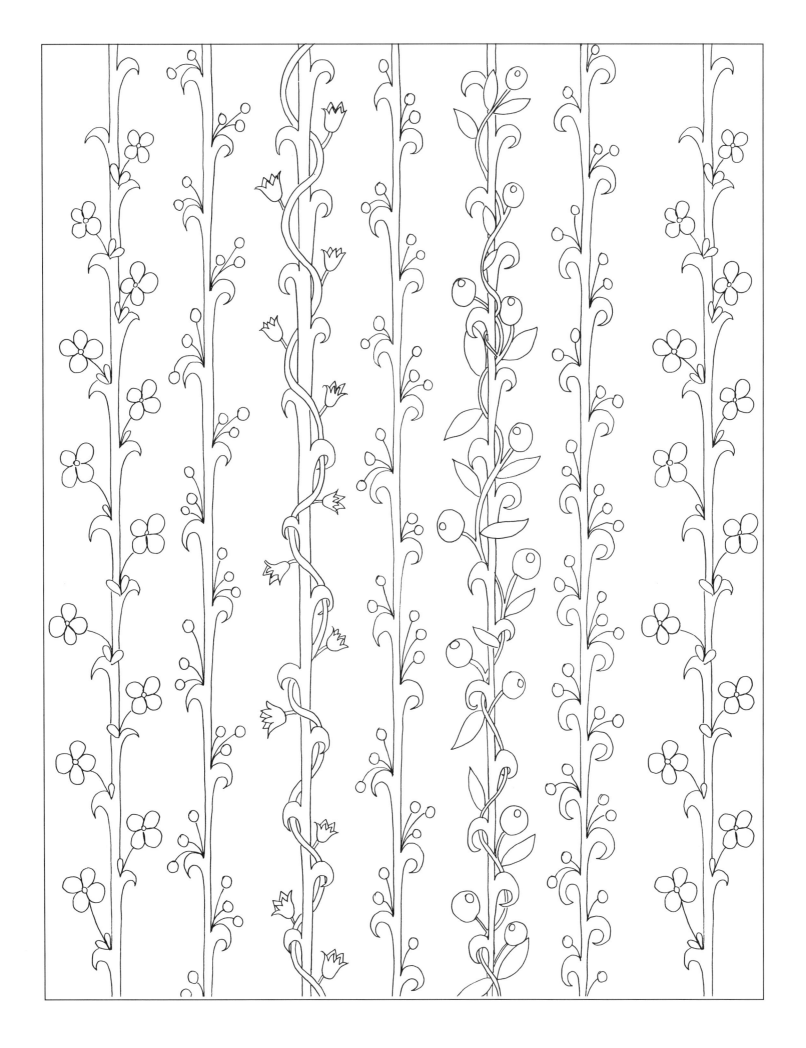

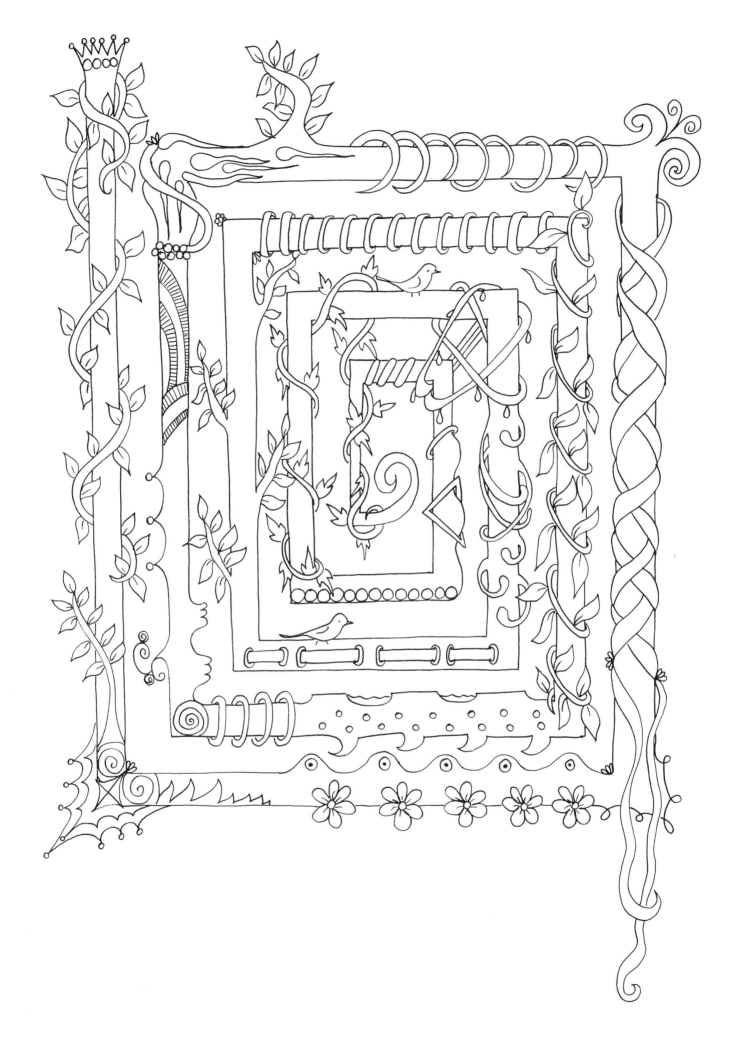